Pressure Cooker Recipes

For

Electric Pressure Cookers

Introduction

Most people think that cooking good food is difficult or time consuming. Some recipes require hours of preparation and many people simply don't have time for that. If you are a fan of food and flavors but don't have hours to spend cooking every day, these pressure cooker recipes might be for you. Pressure cookers utilize high-pressure and high temperatures to speed up the cooking time of food, while allowing the food to retain their nutrient value. Where it may take you an hour and a half to prepare a meal the traditional way, it could take you less than 30 minutes using a pressure cooker. Stop wasting your time and learn how to use a pressure cooker! Start by experimenting with these delicious recipes.

Table of Contents

Perfect....Anything

It's so easy to cook in these pressure cookers that instead of giving you an individual recipe for each thing, I can just tell you the technique, and you can create your own culinary masterpieces.

You can cook any meat or vegetables in your cooker. This recipe will work for pork, turkey, lamb, chicken, beef, or game meats. Just consult the Cooking Time Chart to set the timer. If you want to mix things, try to use meats that have similar cooking times if possible. Otherwise, use the cooking time for the longest cooking ingredient. For game meats, use the closest thing on the timer, ie; Beef for deer, elk, moose, antelope, etc... Chicken for squirrel, rabbit, opossum, doves, quail, etc...

This recipe also works with fish, but you need to wrap the fish in parchment paper so that it won't fall apart. Carp is especially delicious prepared like this. Just season each piece like you want, and add a veggie or two, or a slice of lemon, or lime, if desired, wrap the pieces individually and stack them on the rack, which you set on the vegetables, or other ingredients. When you open the packets (I just slit the paper across the top and serve it in the packet, to hold in the juices), you will be amazed at the tender, moist fish, just full of flavor!

Large pieces of meat, or any roast that will fit in the cooker.
Your favorite vegetables (potatoes, broccoli, carrots, celery, etc...)
Salt, pepper, spices to taste.
2 cups of water
Add water to the cooker.
Add vegetables to the bottom.
Rub meat with your favorite spices.

Place rack on top of veggies (you can omit this step, It really doesn't matter much. It just makes it a little easier to remove the meat after cooking), or set the meat directly on top of veggies.

Set the timer for whatever meat you are cooking. If you are not sure, beef and pork will absolutely cook all the way in 45 minutes to an hour (45 for thawed, 1 hour for frozen), usually a lot less. But 45 minutes will almost always work. Chicken goes about 10-20 minutes, maybe 30 is frozen solid. Turkey roast, about 1 hour, or 90 minutes if frozen. Fish, 5 minutes, or 10 if frozen. You really don't have to worry much about over-cooking in these cookers. They are very forgiving.

When the time is up, either let the pressure reduce on its own, or vent it manually.

Remove the lid, place food on plates, and chow down.....

That's really all there is to it.

Another tip:

Brown your meat in a bit of oil before pressure cooking and this can be done right in the pot in which you apply the pressure. The steam will soften the fibers but it won't brown, so if you're looking for a more appetizing presentation, brown first.

There are many different types of Electric Pressure Cookers. Many of them have different settings and buttons. Some have Meat, Poultry, and Vegetable modes.

These recipes were cooked in a Wolfgang Puck Pressure Cooker that has only 3 options.

Heat, Cook and Warm. I used the Heat mode to saute and brown, and when everything was ready to cook I just set the timer to the required time. If you have a different model you can experiment with the different cooking modes. It should be very easy!

HAPPY COOKING!

Electric pressure cooker Entrees

Beef Pot roast

Ingredients:

- 4 lb. beef steak
- 2 onions, chopped
- 4 garlic cloves
- 2 quart beef stock
- 3 carrots, diced
- 3 celery stalks, roughly chopped
- 1 can diced tomatoes with juice
- ½ tsp. celery seeds
- 2 bay leaves
- 2 tsp. marjoram
- ¼ tsp. dried thyme, crushed
- 1 tsp. cornstarch
- ½ cup water
- Salt and pepper to taste

Method: pressure cooker to heat mode.

Add the onions and garlic into the cooker, followed by the meat.

- Pour the beef stock over the meat and simmer the mixture for a couple of minutes.
- Put the lid on and set the timer to 45 minutes (on "meat" function if possible)
- When the cooker reaches the end of cooking time, release the pressure manually and unlock it.
- Transfer the beef onto a chopping board and chop it into fine strips.
- Toss in the veggies and empty the can of tomatoes into the cooker.
- Stir in seasonings as well as herbs and drop a couple of bay leaves into it; stir well to mix.
- Set to heat mode.
- Dissolve the cornstarch in water until the mixture is free of lumps and stir it into the sauce.
- Simmer the sauce for about 5 minutes, uncovered, until the sauce thickens.
- Divide the beef strips into serving plates and top them up with sauce and veggies.
- Serve immediately.

Braised beef shanks

Serves: 4

Ingredients:

- 4 thick beef shanks
- 6 white button mushrooms, trimmed and quartered
- 1 onion, sliced
- 1 garlic clove, sliced horizontally
- 2 celery ribs, diced
- 1 carrot, peeled and diced
- 1 ¾ cup red wine
- 2 tbsp tomato paste
- 2 tbsp barbeque sauce
- 2 cups chicken broth
- 1 bay leaf
- 2 sprigs fresh thyme
- 1 sprig fresh rosemary
- 1 tsp whole black pepper corns
- 2 tbsp EVOO
- Salt and pepper to taste

Method:

- Tie the bay leaf, sprigs of herbs as well as the peppercorns in a cheese cloth and set aside. This is known as the bouquet garni.
- Rub the salt and pepper all over the meat and toss them into a frying pan, greased with olive oil.
- Brown them for about 10 minutes, flipping them over a number of times and place them into the pressure cooker.

- Skim off 2 tbsp. of the oil from the pan and stir-fry the carrot, onions and celery over moderate heat, for about 5 minute or until the onions softens.
- Add the mushrooms along with a dash of salt and continue to sauté for another couple of minutes, stirring frequently.
- Spoon in the tomato paste along with the garlic and give it a nice stir.
- Simmer the mixture for about 3 minutes or until the sauce darkens few tones darker and add a bout of wine into it.
- Heat the mixture until it starts boiling while stirring at times and place the bouquet garni in the middle of it.
- Continue to boil the mixture for about 7 minutes or until the sauce reduces to half of its previous volume.
- Transfer the mixture into the pressure cooker, along with the barbeque sauce and chicken broth.
- Season with a dash of salt and fasten the lid on the cooker.
- Set the cooker to "meat" function and program the timer to 22 minutes.
- When the time is over, allow the pressure to drop down to normal as per the manufacturer's instructions and open the lid.
- Return the meat and mushrooms back to the frying pan and remove any excess fat from its surface.
- Pour the cooking liquid over the meat and cook over moderate heat until the sauce turns thick and smothers the meat.
- Dish them out into serving plates and serve.

Pulled pork

Serves: 4

Ingredients:

- 1 1/3 lb pork-ribs, chopped into large pieces
- ¼ cup dry sherry
- ¾ cup chicken broth
- 5 oz barbeque sauce
- 1/3 tsp Cajun seasoning
- Salt and pepper to taste

Method:

- Rub the seasoning all over the pork followed by the Cajun seasoning and marinate them in the refrigerator for an hour or more if you can manage.
- Cook the meat in a large pan and cook until they brown on every side.

8

- Add a splash of wine over the meat to glaze them and transfer them to the pressure cooker along with the cooking liquid.
- Pour the chicken broth over the meat and secure the lid.
- Set the timer to 25 minutes.
- Once the cooking time is over, turn off the cooker and open the lid once the pressure is released.
- Strain out the pork and tear them apart with 2 forks.
- Return the pulled pork back into the cooker.
- Pour a little amount of barbeque sauce into the mixture and program the cooker to "warm" mode and stir well.
- Heat the mixture in it for about 15 minutes.
- Pour the meat mixture into a serving bowl and enjoy it with bread or inside sandwiches.

Golden mushroom pork chops

Ingredients:

- 2 lb. pork chops
- 3 cans golden mushrooms
- 1 lb. baby carrots
- 2 cups water
- 1 14 oz. can mushrooms
- Egg noodles, cooked and buttered
- Salt and pepper to taste

Method:

- Empty the can of mushrooms into the pressure cooker along with those of the golden mushrooms.
- Add water and stir well to mix.
- Stir in the carrots and place the pork chops into the cooker.
- Sprinkle a dash of seasonings over it, give the mixture a nice stir and secure lid.

- Set the timer to 20 minutes (in "meat" mode if possible).
- Release the pressure naturally and open the lid.
- Skim off the fat floating on the surface and place the pork chops onto the serving plates.
- Top it up with the carrots and spoon the gravy over them.
- Serve right away.

Whole braised chicken

Serves: 4-6

Ingredients:

- 1 whole chicken, preferably a smaller size so that it can fit into the pressure cooker.
- ½ cup Marsala wine, medium-dry
- 1 tbsp vegetable oil
- 4 cups chicken stock
- 3 cups onion, diced
- 3 cups carrots, diced
- 1 can diced tomatoes
- 6 oz. rotini pasta, uncooked
- 1 tbsp. Worcestershire sauce
- ½ tsp. dried thyme, crushed
- Salt and pepper to taste

Method:

- Bind the chicken firmly with the help of a cotton kitchen cord and cook in the heated vegetable oil, in a pan, until it browns.
- Add the onions as well as carrots to the pan and sauté them until they soften.
- Pour the wine over the chicken to deglaze it and place the chicken into pressure cooker.
- Pour the cooking liquid over it along with the can of tomatoes and its juices.
- Stir in the Worcestershire sauce and sprinkle a dash of seasonings as well as the crushed thyme over the chicken.
- Fasten the lid on the cooker, set it the timer to 25 minutes.

12

- Once the cooking time is over, release pressure manually and open the lid.
- Lift the chicken up from the cooker and untie it.
- Skin the chicken and pull out all the meat from it. Set aside.
- Pour the chicken stock into the cooker.
- Program it back to "heat" function, and bring the mixture to a boil.
- Stir in the pasta and cook, uncovered until cooked properly.
- Turn off the cooker and allow the mixture to cool for about 5 minutes.
- Stir in the pulled chicken, mix and spoon into serving bowls.

Fruity chicken

Ingredients:

- 6 chicken breasts
- 14 oz. peach titbits
- 8 oz. pineapple chunks
- 1 (26 oz.) jar salsa
- 2 chipotle peppers in adobo sauce, finely chopped
- Cooked rice

Method:

- Empty the can of salsa into the pressure cooker along with the pineapple and peach chunks.
- Add the chipotle peppers into the cooker and stir the mixture well,
- Toss the chicken into the cooker and secure the lid.
- Set the timer to 20 minutes (or more in case you decide to use frozen meat).

- Once the cooking time is over, wait until the cooker depressurizes and then unlock it.
- Place the chicken over a bed of rice and spoon the sauce over it.
- Serve right away

Whole chicken with vegetables

Ingredients:

- 1 whole chicken (3-4 lbs.)
- 2 bags frozen vegetables, mixed
- 1 cup chicken broth
- Salt and pepper to taste

Method:

- Rub some seasonings all over the chicken and place it in the pressure cooker.
- Pour the chicken broth over it and empty a bag of frozen veggies into the cook
- Set the cooking time to half an hour.
- Once the cooking cycle is complete, release pressure manually and open lid.
- Add the remaining vegetables and lock the cooker again.
- Set the timer to 5 minutes. Release pressure manually.
  Serve the chicken with rice or pasta.

Coq au vin

Serves: 4

Ingredients:

- 2 lbs. boneless chicken breast, skinned
- 8 oz. white button mushrooms, rinsed and sliced
- 1 large onion, diced
- 28 oz. beef stock
- ½ cup + 2 tbsp. flour
- 1 tsp. Worcestershire sauce
- 1 cup dry red wine
- 2 bay leaves
- 2 tbsp. vegetable oil
- ½ cup water
- Salt and freshly ground pepper to taste

Method:

- Season ½ cup of flour with salt as well as pepper and dust it all over the chicken to coat them well.
- Warm up the empty cooker and drizzle some oil into it.
- Put chicken into the cooker and cook until the chicken browns – 1 or 2 at a time.
- Transfer them to a plate and set aside.
- Throw in the onions into the cooker and sauté them until they are caramelized.
- Stir in the mushrooms and continue to brown them until the juices run out and evaporate.
- Add a splash of wine along with the beef broth into the cooker and drop the bay leaves into it.
- Cook the mixture for about 10 minutes and unplug the cooker to cool it down again.
- Return the chicken to the cooker, switch it on.
- Set timer for 10 minutes then reduce pressure naturally and open lid and remove the chicken.
- Dissolve the remaining flour in ½ cup water and pour it into the broth.
- Give it a nice stir and simmer the mixture until the sauce turns thick.
- Sprinkle the seasonings and pour Worcestershire sauce to the broth.
- Heat the broth for a couple of minutes, uncovered and pour it into a serving bowl.
- Plate and spoon the sauce over the chicken
- Serve right away.

Pot roast

Serves: 6-8

Ingredients:

- 3-4 lbs. chuck roast
- 5 medium potatoes, peeled and quartered
- 1 cup baby carrots, peeled
- 1 cup onion, sliced
- 1 cup celery, chopped
- 2 tsp. beef bouillon powder
- ¼ cup Worcestershire sauce
- 1 ¾ cups water
- 2 bay leaves

19

- 1 tbsp. season-all salt
- ½ tsp. ground black pepper
- 1 tbsp. olive oil

Method:

- Rub the salt all over the meat generously and place it in a pressure cooker.
- Set to heat mode. Drizzle oil into it and heat
- Brown the meat for about 3-4 minutes until it sears evenly and release juices.
- Throw in the celery, carrots and onions into the cooker and sauté them along with the meat, stirring often, until they soften slightly and the meat browns further.
- Pour in water, along with the Worcestershire sauce and drop in the potato quarters.
- Season with a dash of black pepper as well as the bouillon powder and drop in the bay leaves.
- Fasten the lid and set timer for 40 minutes.
- Unplug from heat and set aside until it pressure comes down naturally.
- Open the lid and pour it into a large bowl.
- Serve hot, sliced.

Carne guisada

Serves: 4

Ingredients:

- 1 ½ lb round steaks, trimmed and diced
- ½ onion, sliced
- 1 garlic clove, minced
- 1 fresh tomato, diced
- ½ green bell pepper, diced
- 2 tsp all-purpose flour
- 3 cups water
- ½ cup tomato sauce
- 1 tbsp chili powder
- ¼ tsp dried oregano
- 1 ½ tsp salt
- 1 tsp freshly ground black pepper
- 1 tsp. paprika
- 1 tsp. ground cumin
- 3 tbsp. vegetable oil

21

Method:

- Drizzle oil in a pressure cooker and toss in the meat cubes.
- Brown them in the heat mode, uncovered, for about 3-4 minutes, stirring often, until they are seared evenly and pour in water.
- Sprinkle the ground cumin into the cooker, followed by garlic, dried oregano, paprika, chili powder, tomato sauce and a dash of seasonings.
- Throw in the vegetables and stir them all together to mix well.
- Fasten the lid and set timer for 25 minutes.
- While the meat is cooking, heat a couple of tbsp. oil in a small skillet and dust it with flour.
- Stir the mixture rigorously while cooking it over moderately low heat, until it darkens in color.
- Release the pressure naturally.
- Remove the lid and whisk in the prepared roux until well combined.
- Return the cooker to heat mode and cook further, uncovered, for another 5 minutes or until the careen guisada thickens slightly.
- Serve hot alongside steamed rice.

Meatballs in tomato sauce

Serves: 6

Ingredients:

- 2 lbs. lean ground beef
- 1 can (10 oz.) condensed tomato soup
- 2 tbsp. minced onions
- ½ cup long grain rice, cooked
- ½ cup water
- ¼ tsp. freshly ground black pepper
- ½ tsp. fine salt

Method:

- Place the meat in a large bowl and add the cooked rice into it.
- Sprinkle the onions and a dash of seasonings into it and stir them all together until they are thoroughly distributed throughout the mixture.
- Take portions of this mixture in your hands and roll them into small balls.

23

- Empty the can of tomato soup into a pressure cooker, followed by water and heat it, uncovered, in heat mode until it turns warm; don't let it boil.
- Plop the meatballs into the simmering mixture and fasten the lid to secure.
- Set timer for 8 minutes.
- Remove plug from heat until the pressure comes down naturally.
- Open the lid and serve hot alongside steamed rice or cooked noodles.

Spaghetti in meat sauce

Serves: 6

Ingredients:

- 6 cups spaghetti,
- ½ lb ground beef
- 2 cups fresh mushrooms, sliced
- ½ cup Italian sausage, casing peeled off
- 1 can (28 oz) stewed tomatoes
- 3 garlic cloves, minced
- 1/3 cup fresh parsley, chopped
- 1 onion, finely chopped
- 2 celery stalks, chopped
- 1 cup parmesan cheese, grated
- 1 can (6 oz) tomato paste
- 1 cup chicken broth
- ¼ tsp red pepper flakes, crushed
- 1 tsp dried oregano
- 2 bay leaves
- 1 tsp sugar

25

- Salt and freshly ground black pepper to taste

Method:

- Set the heat mode and brown the sausage meat and beef in a 6 quart pressure cooker, stirring often, until they are just cooked.
- Drain them out, using a slotted spoon into a plate and skim off the rendered fat from the cooker.
- Dump the browned meat back into the pressure cooker, along with the mushrooms, veggies, chicken stock, tomato paste and stewed tomatoes.
- Sprinkle the sugar, crushed red pepper flakes as well as oregano into it and drop in the bay leaves.
- Lock the lid and set timer for 8 minutes while cooking the spaghetti at the same time, in boiling salted water in a separate pot, until cooked al dente.
- Drain pasta out into a colander and keep warm.
- Release the pressure manually.
- Open the lid and discard the bay leaves.
- Pile the spaghetti onto serving plates and spoon the meat sauce over each serving.
- Top it up with a sprinkling of grated parmesan cheese and serve warm.

Beef stroganoff

Serves: 6

Ingredients

- 1 ½ lbs. lean beef chuck, chopped into 1'' chunks
- 12 oz. whole wheat egg noodles
- 2 celery stalks, chopped
- 1 onion, chopped
- 3 carrots, chopped into ½'' chunks
- ¼ cup fresh parsley, coarsely chopped
- 1 lb. whole white button mushrooms
- ¼ cup Neufchatel cheese
- 1 tbsp. all-purpose flour
- 1 cup dry white wine
- 1 cup low-sodium beef broth
- 1 tbsp. Dijon mustard
- 1 tbsp. olive oil
- Salt and freshly ground black pepper to taste

27

Method:

- Sprinkle a dash each of seasonings all over the beef chunks and toss them together to coat well.
- Drizzle a lashing of oil in your pressure cooker in the heat mode.
- Throw in the seasoned beef chunks and brown them for about 4 minutes while stirring at times.
- Stir in the onions and continue to sauté for another 4 minutes, stirring often, until they caramelize and pour in the white wine.
- Dust the flour into the mixture and stir it, along with mustard until well combined.
- Cook the mixture until it starts simmering and continue to do so for a couple of minutes or until the cooking liquid is reduced considerably.
- Pour in the beef broth and toss the mushrooms and rest of the veggies into the cooker.
- Give them a nice stir to mix well and fasten the lid.
- Set the timer for 15 minutes.
- Release the pressure using the quick-release method.
- Once the pressure comes down completely, open the lid carefully and fold in the parsley and cheese; adjust the seasonings.
- Meanwhile, cook the egg noodles in salted boiling water according to the package instructions until cooked al dente.
- Drain them out into a colander and keep warm.
- Pile the noodles onto serving bowls and spoon the beef stroganoff on top of each serving.
- Serve hot.

Giant meatballs in cream sauce

Serves: 6

Ingredients:

- 1 lb. ground beef
- 2 cups fresh porcini mushrooms
- 16 oz. + 1 cup breadcrumbs
- ¼ cup pine nuts
- 3 tsp. parmesan cheese, grated
- 1 cup provolone cheese, diced
- 2 eggs
- 1 ½ cups milk
- 1 tbsp. raisins
- ½ tsp. ground nutmeg
- 1 fresh rosemary sprig
- Salt and freshly ground black pepper
- Olive oil, for cooking

Method:

- Soak 16 oz. breadcrumbs in a bowl with cold water until they soften and give it a tight squeeze to get rid of any excess water in it.
- Place it in a bowl and add the ground beef, raisins, pine nuts, both kinds of cheese, ground nutmeg, salt as well as pepper.
- Crack the eggs into it and stir them all together until well combined.
- Divide the mixture into 2 equal portions and shape each of them into a small loaf.
- Dust them with breadcrumbs until well coated on every side and place them in a pressure cooker.
- Drizzle a lashing of olive oil over them and flip them over several times while cooking them in the heat mode, until they brown evenly.
- Pour in a glass of warm milk, secure the lid and set the timer for 20 minutes. Release pressure.
- Lift the cooked meatloaves carefully out of the cooker and cover them loosely with a tin foil; set aside.
- Set to heat mode and toss the mushrooms into the pressure cooker and pour in remaining milk.
- Throw in the rosemary sprig and sauté mixture, uncovered, for about 10 minutes while stirring often.
- Tip the mixture into a blender and pulse them into a smooth puree.
- Once the loaves are cool enough to handle, slice them into thick slices and drizzle the pureed sauces all over them.

BABOTIE

Serves: 6-8

Ingredients:

- 2 lb ground beef
- 2 onion, finely chopped
- ¼ cup almonds, sliced and toasted
- 1 knob butter
- ½ cup raisins, soaked
- 5 eggs
- 2 slices stale white bread, torn into smaller chunks
- Juice and finely grated zest of 1 lemon
- 1 cup milk
- 4 bay leaves
- ¾ tsp ground turmeric
- 1 tbsp curry powder
- Salt and freshly ground black pepper to taste
- 2 tbsp. Demurer sugar
- 2 tbsp. peanut oil

Method:

- Soak the bread chunks in milk and set aside until they soften.
- Soak the raisins in a separate bowl with boiling water and keep them aside.
- Drizzle the oil in a large saucepan and heat it over moderate flame.
- Throw in the onions and sauté for a while, stirring often, until they soften,
- Sprinkle the spices plus seasonings over them and add the ground beef into it.
- Stir them all together and cook for about 5-7 minutes, stirring at times, until they brown and dry up.
- Give the soaked bread a tight squeeze to get rid of the milk in it and stir it into the mixture.
- Drain the dried fruits into a bowl and set aside.
- Add a splash of lemon juice into it and stir it into the mixture, along with lemon zest, sugar, dried fruits and almonds until well combined.
- Tip the mixture into a greased, heat-proof baking dish and spread it over the base even layer.
- Press it gently to flatten it out and set aside.
- Pour a cup of water into a pressure cooker and place the dish into it making sure that it doesn't touch the sides of the cooker.
- Secure the lid set timer for 10 minutes.
- Meanwhile, to make the topping, crack the eggs into a bowl and whisk in the reserved soaking milk until they blend together to form a pale yellow mixture.
- Once the cooking time is over, allow the pressure to come down naturally and remove the lid.
- Drizzle the egg-milk mixture over the cooked meat and place the bay leaves on top.
- Spread a sheet of foil over the pie and return the dish into the cooker again.
- Place the lid back on, lock set timer for 2 or 3 minutes.
- Release the pressure naturally.
- Serve hot.

Beef Bourguignon

Serves: 5-6

Ingredients:

- 900 gm round steak, chopped into 2 cm chunks
- 3 bacon slices, diced
- 2 garlic cloves, minced
- 2 carrots, chopped into ½ cm slices
- 12 small pearl onion, chopped

  ½ lb. fresh mushrooms, quartered

- ¼ tsp fresh basil
- ½ cup beef stock
- 1 cup dry red wine
- 2 tbsp. all-purpose flour
- Salt and freshly ground black pepper to taste

33

Method:

- Toss the diced bacon into a heated pressure cooker and fry for 2-3 minutes or until they turn crispy golden brown.
- Throw in the onions and continue to stir fry for another couple of minutes.
- Add the beef chunks and sauté them for about 5 minutes, stirring periodically, until they brown nicely.
- Dust the flour into it and give it a nice stir to coat the meat well with it.
- Add a splash of wine into it and pour in the beef stock.
- Sprinkle a dash of seasonings and stir them all together to mix well.
- Secure the lid and set timer for 15 minutes.
- Release the pressure naturally and open the cooker.
- Stir in the mushrooms as well as carrots and put the lid back on.
- Set timer for another 3 minutes, release pressure and tip the mixture into a serving bowl.
- Serve alongside steamed rice or noodles.

Italian beef with green sauce

Serves: 6-8

Ingredients:

For the beef:

- 2 lb. round steak
- 1 small tomato
- 1 medium white onion, skin on and halved
- 1 celery stalk, halved longitudinally
- 1 carrot, cleaned and halved
- 2-3 fresh thyme sprigs
- 1 fresh rosemary sprig
- 1 fresh sage sprig
- 1 tsp whole peppercorns
- 3-8 cloves, inserted into the onion halves
- 1 bay leaf
- 6 cups water
- 3 tbsp. sea salt

For the green sauce:

- ½ cup unseasoned breadcrumbs
- 3 anchovies
- 2 garlic cloves, peeled
- 1 tsp red capers
- 2 bunches fresh parsley, leaves picked
- ½ cup white wine vinegar
- 1 tsp. salt
- Freshly ground black pepper to taste

Method:

- To cook the beef, empty 6 cups water into a pressure cooker set on heat mode and throw in the veggies, bay leaf as well as a dash of salt.
- Tie the herbs together in a bunch and toss it into the cooker.
- Cook the mixture, uncovered in the heat mode until it starts boiling and toss the meat chunks into it.
- Bring the mixture back to a boil and secure the lid.
- Set timer for 25 minutes.
- Allow the pressure to come down naturally and remove the lid.
- Transfer the meat into a dish and continue to simmer the cooking liquid in heat mode, uncovered, for about 5 minutes or until it reduces.
- Tip the reduced broth into a fine mesh sieve to strain into a bowl and leave it in the fridge to cool it down completely.
- Meanwhile, soak the bread crumbs in the vinegar and set aside until they soften.
- Dump rest of the sauce ingredients into a blender and whiz them into a smooth puree.
- Squeeze out the liquid from the soaked breadcrumbs and dunk them into the blender.
- Pulse further while drizzling more olive oil into it until all the ingredients blend together and the sauce reaches desired thickness.
- Scrape it out into a serving bowl and set aside.
- Skim off the fat floating on the surface of the chilled broth and set aside.

- Carve outs semi-thick slices from the beef and arrange them over a serving dish.
- Add splashes of the broth to moisten them up and serve alongside the green sauce.

Thai red curry

Serves:

Ingredients:

- 3 lb beef chuck roast, trimmed and chopped into 2'' chunks
- 1 large red bell pepper, top chopped off, deseeded and coarsely chopped
- 2 medium white onions, quartered
- 4-6 red potatoes
- 2 tbsp. dried basil
- 1 tbsp. fish sauce
- 1 tbsp. dark soy sauce
- 1 can (14 oz) coconut milk
- 1 jar (4 oz) thai red curry paste
- 1 tbsp. brown sugar
- 1 cup water
- 1 tbsp. olive oil
- 1 tsp. sea salt

Method:

- Heat olive oil in a pressure cooker and throw in the peppers well as onions. (on heat mode)
- Sauté them for about 5 minutes, stirring often, until they are seared and drain them out into a bowl.
- Skim off the cream from the surface of the coconut milk and add the former into the cooker.
- Cook for half a minute to deglaze base of the cooker and empty the entire jar of curry paste into it.
- Stir them all together to mix well and cook the mixture for about 5 minutes, while stirring often, until it bubbles begins to appear in it and turn fragrant.
- Pour in the coconut milk, both the sauces and empty a cup of water into it.
- Sprinkle the brown sugar as well as basil into it and stir them all together until well combined.
- Toss the beef chunks into it, followed by a layer of red potatoes on top and fasten the lid.
- Set timer for 10 minutes.
- Bring the pressure down by natural pressure release method and remove the lid.
- Tip the curry into a large serving bowl and serve alongside steamed rice.

Lamb shanks in garlic-wine sauce

Serves: 2

Ingredients:

- 2 lb. lamb shanks, fat trimmed
- 10 garlic cloves, peeled
- 1 tbsp tomato paste
- ½ cup chicken broth
- ½ tsp dried rosemary
- ½ cup port wine
- 1 tsp. balsamic vinegar
- 1 tbsp. olive oil
- 1 tbsp. unsalted butter
- Salt and pepper to taste

Method:

- Rub the seasoning all over the lamb shanks and set aside.
- Drizzle oil in the pressure cooker in heat mode and add the meat as soon as the oil heats up.

40

- Brown the shanks thoroughly and then drop the whole garlic cloves into the cooker to saute them until they brown slightly.
- Pour in the broth and wine along with the rosemary as well as the tomato paste and stir them all together to mix well.
- Set timer for 25 minutes.
- Release pressure manually. (pressure valve) Open lid.
- Transfer the lamb shanks to serving plates and heat the liquid in the cooker, uncovered, until it begins to boil.
- Cook the sauce until it reduces in volume and thickens.
- Whisk the butter and vinegar together in a small mixing bowl and stir it into the sauce.
- Spoon the sauce over the lamb and serve

Mensaf

Serves: 8

Ingredients:

- 2 cups white rice, uncooked
- 2 lb. lamb shoulder, boneless and chopped into 2'' chunks
- 1 cup goat's milk, salted
- ¼ cup pine nuts
- 4 tbsps. olive oil
- 8 cups water
- 6 pita bread rounds

Method:

- Pour a tbps. of oil in your stove-top pressure cooker and heat it in heat mode.
- Throw in the lamb chunks and sauté for about 5 minutes, stirring regularly, until they brown evenly.
- Drain them out onto a plate and place a cooling rack within the cooker.

- Arrange the meat onto a cooker and empty 4 cups of water into it.
- Fasten the lid.
- Set timer for 30 minutes.
- Release pressure naturally.
- Transfer the meat to a plate and remove the flesh from the bones using a couple of forks; keep warm and get rid of the bones.
- Reserve the cooking liquid in a separate bowl and keep it aside until required.
- Pour rest of the water into a saucepan and drizzle another tbsps. of oil into it.
- Add the rice and bring the mixture to a boil over moderately high flame.
- Give it nice stir, place a lid on top and reduce it to a simmer.
- Continue to cook likewise for about 20 minutes, until all the cooking liquid disappears.
- Heat rest of the oil in another skillet over moderate flame and fry the pine nuts in it for about 5 minutes, stirring often, until they turn deep brown in color.
- Empty 2 cups of the reserved cooking liquid into a separate pan and whisk in the goat's milk until well combined.
- Toss the lamb shreds into the above mixture and bring it to a simmer.
- Continue to cook over moderate heat for about half an hour or until most of the liquid is absorbed by the meat.
- To serve, place the pita breads onto a large plate and pile the rice on top of them.
- Scatter the shredded lamb on top of the rice and smother them with rest of the milk sauce.
- Finish it off with a sprinkling of pine nuts and serve right away.

Chicken cacciatore

Serves: 4

Ingredients:

- 3 lbs. skinless chicken breast, halved
- 1 green bell pepper, seeded and diced
- 10 oz. mushrooms, sliced
- 2 cups tomatoes, crushed
- 3 garlic cloves, chopped
- 3 shallots, chopped
- ½ cup white wine
- 2 tsp. tomato paste
- ½ cup parmesan cheese, grated
- 2 tbsps. red pepper flakes, crushed
- 2 tbsps. fresh parsley, finely chopped
- 6 oz. kalamata olives, drained
- 1 tbsps. olive oil
- Salt and black pepper to taste

Method:

- Set pressure cooker on heat mode and sauté the shallots as well as bell pepper for a couple of minutes, stirring them all the time.
- Once the shallots soften, pour a splash of wine into it and boil the mixture until it reduces to half its previous volume.
- Throw in the garlic as well as mushrooms and arrange the chicken breasts over them.
- Top the chicken with the crushed tomatoes and pour the tomato paste over them.
- Refrain from any stirring and secure the lid.
- Set timer for 8 minutes.
- Let the pressure drop down naturally.
- Unlock the cooker and stir in the remaining ingredients.
- Transfer it into a serving bowl and serve over a bed of cooked pasta or white rice.

Tortellini and chicken with cream-cheese sauce

Serves: 6

Ingredients:

- 4 boneless chicken breasts, skin removed
- 3 bacon slices, cut into pieces
- 8 oz. cheese-filled tortellini
- 4 oz. mushrooms, roughly chopped
- 4 shallots, minced
- 1 lbs. asparagus, trimmed and sliced into 2'' pieces
- 1small carrot, finely sliced
- 1/3 cup parmesan cheese
- 2 tsp. corn starch
- ¼ cup + 3 tbsp. butter, softened
- ½ cup half and half
- 2 cups chicken broth
- 1 tsp. dried tarragon
- 3 tbsps. dry parsley flakes

Method:

- Fry the bacon on heat mode in the pressure cooker for a couple of minutes before stirring in the onions, parsley as well as ¼ cup butter and stir-fry them for another 2 minutes.
- Add the chicken along with mushrooms, carrots and tarragon into the pressure cooker and empty the cups of broth into it.
- Mix them well by stirring and lock the cooker.
- Set timer for 6 minutes.
- Let the pressure drop by releasing it naturally and unlock it.
- Add the asparagus, secure the lid and set timer for 2 more minutes and remove the lid again after releasing the pressure.
- Meanwhile, whisk remaining butter and cheese into the half and half and pour it into the chicken-tortellini mixture.
- Give it a gentle stir and cook briefly over moderate flame until the sauce becomes creamy and thick.
- Pour the mixture into serving plates and serve.

Chicken Piccata

Serves: 6

Ingredients:

- 3 chicken breast, each cut into halves
- ¼ cup parmesan cheese, grated
- ¼ cup sour cream
- ½ cup+ 1 tbsps. all-purpose flour
- 3 garlic cloves, crushed
- 4 shallots
- 1 cup pimento stuffed olive, minced
- 1 tsp. dried basil
- ¼ tsp. white pepper
- 2 tsps. salt
- ¾ cup chicken broth
- ¼ cup olive oil
- 1 tbsps. sherry wine
- 1/3 cup fresh lemon juice

Method:

- Dredge the chicken breast halves with flour.
- Heat oil in heat mode and brown the chicken in batches, flipping them over a number of times; set aside.
- Sauté the garlic and shallots in the cooker before adding a splash of lemon juice and sherry to the mixture.
- Stir in the broth along with the olives, basil as well as seasonings and cook briefly.
- Place the chicken back into the cooker, with the skin side facing down and place the lid.
- Set timer for 10 minutes.
- Release the pressure and open the lid.
- Stir the mixture a couple of times and spoon the chicken into the serving plate.
- Whisk a tbsps. Of flour into the sour cream and stir it into the sauce.
- Simmer the sauce for a minute while stirring continuously, until it thickens and spoon it over the chicken.
- Top the chicken up with cheese and serve.

Hungarian chicken

Serves: 4

Ingredients:

- 4 lb. chicken leg quarters, bone-in and skin removed
- 1 medium tomato, peeled and coarsely chopped
- 1 small onion, finely chopped
- ½ cup sour cream
- 2 tsps. hot Hungarian paprika
- ½ cup chicken broth
- 1 tsps. salt
- 1 tbsp. olive oil
- 6 Oz wide egg noodles, cooked al dente, drained and greased with butter

Method:

- Drizzle oil in your pressure cooker set in heat mode and heat.

- Toss the chicken pieces into it and sauté for about 4-5 minutes, stirring at times, until they turn golden brown in color; drain them out onto a plate and set aside until necessary.
- Throw in the onions and season with a dash of paprika.
- Pour in the broth and give it a nice stir until well combined.
- Plop the chicken back into the cooker, along with the tomato chunks and sprinkle a dash of salt on top.
- Secure the lid and set timer for 7 minutes.
- Let it rest for about 5 minutes and release any pressure within the cooker.
- Open the lid and drain the chicken out into a plate.
- Place the lid back on and set the cooker to heat mode for about 15 minutes to let the liquid cook further in the heat trapped inside.
- Pour ¼ cup of the cooking liquid into a bowl and beat in the sour cream until well mixed.
- Return the mixture into the cooker and whisk it thoroughly until it blend into the liquid properly.
- Return the cooked chicken back into the cooker and cook, uncovered, over moderate heat until heated through.
- Pile the cooked noodles at the center of the serving plate and place the chicken pieces on top.
- Drizzle the sauce over them and serve warm.

Chicken in Sweet Onion Sauce

Serves: 6

Ingredients:

- 6 boneless chicken breasts, skinned
- 1 lb. baby carrots
- 2 large sweet onions, peeled and diced
- 8 oz. fresh mushrooms, sliced
- 6 medium potatoes, peeled and sliced
- 1 can (10 ¾ oz.) cream of mushroom soup
- 2 tbsps. heavy cream
- 1 tbsps. butter
- 1 tbsps. olive oil

Method:

- Se pressure cooker to heat mode.
- Throw in the onions and stir fry for a couple of minutes or until soft.
- Dump the mushrooms and continue to stir fry for another 3 minutes.

52

- Arrange the chicken breasts on top of the sautéed mixture and scatter the vegetables into it.
- Empty the can of mushroom soup and secure the lid.
- Set timer for 10 minutes.
- Wait until the pressure comes down naturally.
- Open the cooker and drain the chicken as well as the veggies out into a large serving bowl.
- Return the cooker to heat mode and whisk in the cream until well combined.
- Bring it to a simmer and continue to do so until it thickens slightly.
- Drizzle the sauce over the veggie-chicken mixture and serve hot.

Teriyaki chicken

Serves: 2

Ingredients:

For the teriyaki sauce:

- 2 cups cold water
- ½ cup soy sauce
- ½ cup sugar
- ¼ tsp. garlic, crushed
- 2 tbsps. cornstarch

For the chicken:

- 2 cups teriyaki sauce
- 2 large chicken breasts, boneless and skinned

Method:

- To make the teriyaki sauce, whisk all its ingredients together until well combined and the sugar dissolves.
- Pour it into a saucepan and cook over moderate heat until it starts boiling.
- Continue to boil for a couple of minutes or until it thickens and tip it into a bowl
- Or use premade sauce.
- Place the chicken breasts in the bowl, and flip it over to coat either sides with the sauce.
- Place a lid on top and leave in the fridge for about 30 minutes to marinate.
- Transfer the marinated chicken into your pressure cooker and fasten the lid.
- Set timer for 12 minutes. Release pressure naturally.
- Lift the chicken out into a plate and set aside until cool enough to handle.
- Tear it into shreds with your fingers or a fork and pile it up onto a serving platter.
- Cook the sauce further for another 5-8 minutes, uncovered, until it thickens and pour it over the shredded chicken.
- Serve right away.

Mushroom chicken

Serves: 6

Ingredients:

- 2 lb. boneless chicken breasts, skinned
- 8 oz. button mushrooms, halved
- 3 garlic cloves, sliced
- 1 onion, chopped
- 2 tbsps. Dijon mustard
- ¾ cup chicken broth
- 2 cans cream of mushroom soup
- 1 tsp. dried thyme
- 1/8 tsp freshly ground black pepper
- ½ tsp. salt
- 3 tbsps. olive oil

Method:

- Heat the oil in a pressure cooker on heat mode and place the chicken breasts in it, a couple of them at a time.
- Cook them for about 5 minutes, uncovered, while flipping them over in the middle of cooking to brown either sides evenly and drain them out into a plate.
- Crush the dried thyme onto the browned chicken and season with a dash of salt as well as pepper.
- Rub the seasonings all over the chicken and set aside.
- Throw in the mushrooms, garlic and onions into the pressure cooker and stir fry for about 3-5 minutes or until they soften.
- Arrange the seasoned chicken breasts on top of the sautéed layer and empty the can of mushrooms soup into it, followed by mustard and broth.
- Stir them all together to mix well and fasten the lid to secure.
- Set timer for 10 minutes.
- Release pressure manally.
- Remove the lid and give it a final stir to mix thoroughly.
- Serve on top of cooked, hot pasta.

Chicken tagine

Serves: 6

Ingredients:

- 2 lbs. boneless chicken breasts, skinned and chopped into bit-sized chunks
- 2 garlic cloves, peeled and minced
- 2 large onions, peeled and diced
- 2 tsp. fresh ginger root, grated
- 12 large green olives, pitted
- 2 tbsps. fresh flat-leaf parsley, minced
- 1 lemon
- 2 tsp. cold water
- 2 tbsps. cornstarch
- 2 tbsps. honey
- 2 cups chicken broth
- ½ tsp. saffron threads
- 1 tsp ground cumin

- Salt and freshly ground black pepper to taste
- 1 tbsps. extra virgin olive oil
- 2 tbsps. butter

Method:

- Add the butter into the pressure cooker and drizzle the oil into it.
- Heat on heat mode until the butter melts and throw in the onions.
- Stir fry for about 2-3 minutes and stir in the ginger, garlic and the spices.
- Sauté the mixture briskly for half a minute and toss the chicken chunks into the cooker.
- Sauté for another 1 minute, stirring often and empty the cups of broth into it.
- Grate the zest of half of the lemon into it, followed by a splash of freshly squeezed out lemon juice and honey.
- Close the lid. Set timer for 8 minutes.
- Release the pressure by the quick-release method and unlock the lid.
- Add the olives and grated zest of rest of the lemon and give it a nice stir to mix well.
- Whisk the cornstarch in cold water until it forms a smooth mixture and beat it into the chicken mixture until well combined.
- Simmer the mixture, uncovered, for about 3 minutes, stirring often, until it thickens and raw smell of the cornstarch disappears.
- Add in the parsley until well combined and adjust the seasonings.
- Serve hot.

Chicken And Spinach Curry

Serves: 6

Ingredients:

- 1 lb. boneless chicken breasts, skinned and chopped into 1' chunks
- 6 cups cooked rice
- 2 (10 oz. each) packages frozen spinach, thawed
- 2 tbsps. apple sauce
- ½ cup chicken broth
- 1 tbsps. mild curry powder
- 1 ½ cups packaged pasta sauce
- Salt and freshly ground black pepper to taste
- Chopped fresh cilantro, for garnishing

Method:

- Toss the chicken pieces into the pressure cooker and pour in the broth.

- Scatter the spinach leaves on top and set aside.
- Whisk the curry powder into the pasta sauce until well mixed and drizzle it over the spinach.
- Don't stir and secure the lid.
- Set timer for 6 minutes.
- Release the pressure by fast release method and unlock the cooker.
- Spoon in the applesauce and stir them all together to mix well.
- Simmer the sauce, uncovered, for about 5 minutes or until the sauce thickens slightly and adjust the seasonings.
- Pile up the cooked rice onto serving plates and top it up with the chicken curry.
- Sprinkle the chopped cilantro over each serving and serve warm.

Chicken chili

Serves: 4

Ingredients:

- 2 lb. boneless chicken thighs, skinned and chopped into bite-sized chunks
- 1 can (16 oz.) red kidney beans, washed and drained
- 1 garlic clove, minced
- 1 red bell pepper, deseeded and cubed
- 1 can (15 oz.) diced tomatoes
- 1 small yellow onion, diced
- 1 jalapeno pepper, deseeded and minced
- 1 tbsps. tomato paste
- 1 tsp. chili powder
- 1 tbsps. paprika
- ¼ tsp. dried oregano
- ¼ tsp. dried thyme
- 1 tbsps. tomato paste
- 2 tbsps. vegetable oil

62

- Salt and freshly ground black pepper to taste

Method:

- Heat oil in a pressure cooker on heat mode and put the chicken chunks into it.
- Sauté for about 2 minutes, stirring at times, until they brown slightly and stir in the red peppers as well as jalapeno.
- Continue to sauté for another minute, stirring often and throw in the onions.
- Empty the can of diced tomatoes as well as kidney beans.
- Add the garlic and tomato paste into the mixture and sprinkle the paprika, dried herbs, chili powder as well as a dash of seasonings.
- Pour in the broth and stir them all together to mix well.
- Secure the lid and set timer for 10 minutes.
- Bring the pressure down by quick release method and give the chili a final stir until well combined; adjust the seasonings.
- Scoop the chili into a serving bowl and serve hot.

Spanish rice with chicken

Serves: 4

Ingredients:

- 1 lb. boneless chicken breasts, skinned and chopped into bite-sized chunks
- 4 oz. fresh cremini mushrooms, cleaned and sliced
- 1 cup long-grain rice, uncooked
- 1 large green bell pepper, deseeded and diced
- 1 white onions, peeled and diced
- ½ cup black olives, pitted and halved
- 2 garlic cloves, peeled and minced
- 1 tsp. chili powder
- 1/8 tsp. dried oregano
- ¼ tsp. dried thyme
- ¼ tsp. freshly ground black pepper
- 1 tsp. smoked paprika
- Pinch of cayenne pepper
- 2 cups chicken broth
- 2 tbsps. vegetable oil

Method:

- Heat the oil in the pressure cooker in heat mode and toss the chicken chunks into it, along with the onion plus bell pepper.
- Sprinkle the dried herbs, chili powder, cayenne, black pepper as well as paprika over them and sauté for about 3 minutes, stirring periodically, until the chicken browns and the onions soften.
- Dump the mushrooms into it and stir fry for another couple of minutes.
- Stir in the garlic and olives and add the rice into it.
- Pour in the broth and fasten the lid and set timer for minutes.
- Let it rest for about 7-10 minutes to allow the pressure to come down naturally and remove the lid.
- Stir the chicken-rice mixture all together to mix well and adjust the seasonings.
- Serve hot.

Jambalaya

Serves: 4-6

Ingredients:

- ½ lb. boneless chicken breasts, skinned and chopped into 1'' chunks
- ½ lb. uncooked shrimp, peeled and deveined
- ½ lb. fully cooked Andouille sausage, sliced
- 1 cup long grain white rice
- 3 garlic cloves, minced
- 3 celery stalks, sliced
- 1 onion, chopped
- 1 green bell pepper, chopped
- 3 tbsp. fresh parsley, minced
- 1 can (16 oz.) chopped tomatoes, drained and juice reserved
- 1/8 tsp. cayenne pepper
- 1 tsp. dried thyme
- 2 tsp. creole seasoning
- 1 cup chicken stock
- 1 tbsp. vegetable oil

66

Method:

- Heat oil in a pressure cooker on heat mode and throw in the shrimps, sausage and chicken chunks.
- Sprinkle half each of the thyme, creole seasoning and cayenne pepper into the cooker and give the ingredients a good stir to coat well with the seasonings.
- Sauté for about 3 minutes, uncovered, stirring often, until the shrimps and chicken are cooked through.
- Drain them out, using a slotted spoon into a plate and keep them aside until necessary.
- Dump the veggies into the cooker and sprinkle rest of the thyme, cayenne pepper and creole seasoning all over them.
- Sauté for another 3 minutes, uncovered, while stirring regularly, until the veggies are just cooked yet retain their crispness.
- Empty the cup of rice into it, followed by stock as well as the canned tomatoes including their juice.
- Place the lid on top. Lock set timer for 8 minutes.
  Release the pressure slowly.
- Open the lid and return the sautéed meat and shrimps back into the cooker.
- Sprinkle the parsley leaves on top and stir them all together to mix well.
- Place the lid back on and let it rest for 5 minutes.
- Pile it up into serving dishes and serve warm.

Shrimp risotto

Serves: 4

Ingredients:

- 1 ½ cups Arborio rice
- 1 lb. medium shrimp, peeled and deveined
- 1 small Vidalia onion, diced
- 3 garlic cloves, minced
- 1 tsp. fennel seeds
- Salt and freshly ground black pepper to taste
- Pinch of saffron threads
- 3 cups chicken broth
- 2 tbsp. tomato paste
- ¼ cup dry white vermouth
- 2 tbsp. extra virgin olive oil

Method:

- Heat oil in the pressure cooker in heat mode until it's hot and throw in the onions.

- Sprinkle the fennel seeds into it and stir fry for about 3 minutes or until the onion softens but doesn't change color.
- Empty the cups of rice into it and stir it into the sautéed mixture along with garlic, saffron and tomato paste.
- Add a splash of vermouth as well as broth and give it another stir to mix well.
- Fasten the lid set timer for 15 minutes.
- Allow the pressure to come down by quick release method and open the lid.
- Return the cooker back to heat mode and toss the shrimps into it.
- Stir them into the cooked rice and stir.
- Cook likewise for a couple of minutes or until the flesh of the shrimps turn opaque and they are thoroughly cooked.
- Adjust the seasonings and serve right away.

Beef Masala

Servings: 4 to 5

Ingredients:

- 2 lbs. round steak, cut into chunks
- ½ lbs. sliced mushrooms
- 1 onion, chopped
- 1 green pepper, sliced thin
- ½ cup all-purpose flour
- ½ cup Masala wine
- 2 tbsp. tomato paste
- 2 tbsp. unsalted butter
- Salt and pepper to taste

Instructions:

1. Place the chunks of steak between pieces of plastic wrap and flatten with a meat mallet to about ¼-inch thick. Season the meat with black pepper.
2. Mix the flour and salt in a plastic bag and add the meat. Shake to coat.
3. Melt the butter in the pressure cooker on the "heat or brown" setting.
4. Add the beef and cook until browned. Remove from the cooker.
5. Stir in the onions, mushrooms and peppers. Cook for 3 minutes.
6. Add the masala wine and stir to deglaze the pan. Cook for 1 minute.
7. Mix in the tomato paste and about 1 cup water. Return the meat to the cooker and close and lock the lid on the pressure cooker.
8. Set timer for 15 minutes.
9. Allow the cooker to depressurize naturally then remove the lid. Serve the beef with the sauce on the side.

Tomato-Garlic and Beef Sauce

Servings: 6

Ingredients:

- 2 lbs. round steak
- 2 tbsp. olive oil
- 1 (28 oz.) can crushed tomatoes
- ½ cup red wine
- ¼ cup grated Parmesan
- 2 tbsp. minced garlic
- 1 tbsp. dried oregano
- 1 tsp. dried basil
- Salt and pepper to taste

Instructions:

1. Heat the oil in the pressure cooker on the "heat" setting. Add the beef and cook until browned. Set aside.

2. Remove the fat and deglaze the cooker with the red wine, stirring well.
3. Add in the parmesan, tomatoes, garlic and spices. Add the meat and stir to combine.
4. Close and lock the lid on the pressure cooker and set timer for5 minutes.
5. Allow the cooker to depressurize naturally then remove the lid. Serve the beef with pasta and the sauce on the side.

Braised Beef in Red Wine Sauce

Servings: 4 to 5

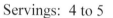

Ingredients:

- 3 lbs. beef chuck roast
- 2 tbsp. olive oil
- 2 tbsp. minced garlic
- 1 cup chopped carrots
- 2 onions, chopped
- 1 cup fresh chopped parsley
- ½ cup all-purpose flour
- ½ cup light red wine
- 1 (28 oz.) can Italian stewed tomatoes
- 1 cup beef broth
- 1 tsp. dried oregano
- 1 tsp. dried rosemary

- Salt and pepper to taste

Instructions:

1. Mix the salt, pepper and flour in a plastic bag. Add the beef and shake to coat it evenly.
2. Heat the olive oil in the pressure cooker on the "heat" setting. Add the meat and cook until evenly browned. Remove from cooker.
3. Stir in the onions and garlic, cooking for 2 minutes or until tender.
4. Add the wine and stir to deglaze the bottom of the cooker.
5. Put the meat back in the cooker and add the remaining ingredients. Stir well.
6. Close and lock the lid on the pressure cooker and set timer for 30 minutes.
7. Allow the pressure to release naturally and remove the lid.
8. Shred the beef with two forks and serve hot with the vegetables and sauce.

Steak Pizzaiola

Servings: 6

Ingredients:

- 2 lbs. flank steak, sliced
- ½ lbs. sliced mushrooms
- 2 tbsp. olive oil
- 1 onion, sliced
- 2 bell peppers, chopped
- 1 (14 oz.) can crushed tomatoes
- 1 tbsp. minced garlic
- 2 tsp. dried basil
- Salt and pepper to taste

Instructions:

1. Heat the oil in the pressure cooker on the "heat" setting. Add the sliced beef and cook until browned. Set aside.
2. Add the onions and cook until softened, about 2 minutes.
3. Add in the mushrooms, tomatoes, garlic, peppers and spices. Stir to combine.
4. Return the meat to the pressure cooker and close and lock the lid in place.
5. Set timer for 20 minutes. Allow the cooker to depressurize naturally.
6. Remove the lid and stir. Serve hot.

Chicken Roman

Servings: 6

Ingredients:

- 6 boneless chicken breasts
- ½ cup all-purpose flour
- 2 tbsp. olive oil
- 1 onion, diced
- 1 (4 oz.) can mushrooms, drained
- 1 (10 oz.) can tomato sauce
- 1 tbsp. white sugar
- 1 tbsp. minced garlic
- 1 tbsp. Italian seasoning
- 1 tsp. vinegar
- 1 tsp. chicken bouillon granules
- Salt and pepper to taste

- 1 cup grated Parmesan

Instructions:

1. Mix the salt, pepper and flour in a plastic bag. Add the chicken and shake to coat it evenly.
2. Heat the olive oil in the pressure cooker on the "heat" setting. Add the chicken and cook until evenly browned. Remove from cooker.
3. Stir in the onions and garlic, cooking for 3 minutes or until tender.
4. Add the tomato sauce, vinegar, sugar, mushrooms, bouillon and spices. Stir in ½ cup water.
5. Return the chicken to the cooker2 Close and lock the lid in place.
6. Set the pressure cooker for 10 minutes. Allow the cooker to depressurize naturally.
7. Remove the lid and transfer the chicken to a platter.
8. Serve hot garnished with grated Parmesan.

Lemon Chicken with Herbs

Servings: 6

Ingredients:

- 4 boneless chicken breasts, cubed
- ¼ cup white wine
- 2 tbsp. olive oil
- 2 tbsp. fresh lemon juice
- 2 tsp. minced garlic
- 2 tsp. chicken bouillon granules
- 1 tbsp. fresh chopped basil
- 1 tbsp. fresh chopped oregano
- Salt and pepper to taste

Instructions:

1. Heat the olive oil in the pressure cooker on the "heat" setting. Add the chicken and cook until evenly browned. Set aside.
2. Stir in the remaining ingredients and close and lock the lid in place.
3. Set the pressure 10 minutes. Release pressure manually.
4. Remove the lid and transfer the chicken to a platter.
5. Simmer the sauce on the "heat" setting for 5 minutes or until slightly thickened. Serve hot with the chicken.

Basil Tomato Chicken

Servings: 4

Ingredients:

- 4 boneless chicken breasts
- 2 tbsp. olive oil
- 1 chopped onion
- 1 (28 oz.) can Italian stewed tomatoes
- ¼ cup fresh chopped basil
- 2 tsp. minced garlic
- Salt and pepper to taste

Instructions:

1. Rub the chicken with pepper and salt on both sides.

2. Heat the olive oil in the pressure cooker on the "heat" setting. Add the chicken and cook until evenly browned. Set aside.
3. Put in the garlic and onions, stir and cook for 2 minutes or until tender.
4. Add the remaining ingredients and return the chicken to the cooker. Close and lock the lid in place.
5. Set timer for 8 minutes. Allow the cooker to depressurize naturally.
6. Remove the lid and transfer the chicken to a platter.
7. Serve hot with the sauce on the side.

Balsamic Chicken

Servings: 6

Ingredients:

- 6 boneless chicken breasts
- 1/3 cup balsamic vinegar
- 1/3 cup chicken broth
- 2 tbsp. olive oil
- 1 tbsp. minced garlic
- 2 tsp. lemon pepper seasoning

Instructions:

1. Place the chicken breasts between two sheets of plastic wrap and flatten gently with a meat mallet.
2. Rub the chicken with the lemon pepper seasoning on both sides.

3. Heat the olive oil in the pressure cooker on the "heat" setting. Add the chicken and cook until evenly browned. Set aside.
4. Deglaze the pan with the chicken broth and add the remaining ingredients and stir. Add the chicken back to the cooker. Close and lock the lid in place.
5. Set the pressure cooker to 10 minutes. Allow the cooker to depressurize naturally.
6. Remove the lid and transfer the chicken to a platter.
7. Simmer the sauce on the "heat" setting for 10 minutes or until slightly thickened if needed Serve hot with the chicken.

Chicken Cacciatore

Servings: 4 to 6

Ingredients:

- 8 boneless chicken thighs
- 2 tbsp. olive oil
- 2 onions, sliced
- 2 cups sliced mushrooms
- ½ cup sliced olives
- 1 (16 oz.) jar pasta sauce
- 1 tbsp. minced garlic
- 1 tbsp. Italian seasoning
- Salt and pepper to taste

Instructions:

1. Place the chicken thighs between two sheets of plastic wrap and flatten gently with a meat mallet.
2. Rub the chicken with salt and pepper to taste.
3. Heat the olive oil in the pressure cooker on the "heat" setting. Add the chicken and cook until evenly browned. Set aside.
4. Add the mushrooms and onions. Cook, stirring, for 3 minutes.
5. Add in the remaining ingredients including the chicken and stir. Close and lock the lid tightly in place.
6. Set the pressure cooker timer for 8 minutes. Allow the cooker to depressurize naturally.
7. Remove the lid and transfer the chicken to a platter. Serve hot.

Roasted Chicken

Servings: 4 to 5

Ingredients:

- 1 (2 to 3 lbs.) whole roasting chicken
- 1 cup water
- 1 tbsp. minced garlic
- 1 tbsp. Italian seasoning
- 3 sprigs fresh rosemary
- Salt and pepper to taste

Instructions:

1. Place a rack inside the pressure cooker and pour in the water.

2. Remove the giblets from the chicken and rinse under cold water. Pat the chicken dry with paper towels.
3. Stuff the garlic and rosemary into the cavity of the chicken and season the skin with salt, pepper and Italian seasoning.
4. Tuck the wings under the chicken and tie the legs together with string. Set the chicken on the rack.
5. Close and lock the lid in place set timer for 20 minutes.
6. Allow the cooker to depressurize naturally and check the temperature of the chicken – if it is 170°F or more, it is done.
7. Cook for 5 minutes more, if needed.
8. For a crispy skin, preheat the oven to 450°F and place the chicken in a roasting pan. Roast for 15 minutes until golden brown.
9. Let rest for 10 minutes before carving.

Simple Chicken in Red Wine Sauce

Servings: 4

Ingredients:

- 4 boneless chicken breasts
- 2 cups button mushrooms
- ½ lbs. bacon
- 1 chopped onion
- 2 cups red wine
- 1 (14 oz.) can chicken broth
- 1 tsp. Italian seasoning

Instructions:

1. Cook the bacon in the pressure cooker on the "heat" setting until crisp. Set aside on paper towels to drain.

2. Add the garlic and onion to the pressure cooker and cook until softened, about 3 minutes. Drain on paper towels.
3. Add the mushrooms, stirs and cook until softened then set aside to drain.
4. Brown the chicken breasts in the pressure cooker then remove and drain the fat from the cooker.
5. Return the cooked ingredients to the cooker and add the remaining ingredients. Close and lock the lid.
6. Set pressure cooker timer for 10 minutes. Manually release the pressure.
7. Remove the lid and transfer the chicken to a platter.
8. Simmer the sauce on the "brown" setting for 10 minutes or until slightly thickened (if needed) Serve hot with the chicken.

Linguine Chicken Alfredo

Servings: 4

Ingredients:

- 1 stick butter, softened
- 1 cup heavy cream
- ¾ cups grated Parmesan
- 4 boneless chicken breasts
- 2 tbsp. olive oil
- 1 chopped onion
- 1 chopped red pepper
- ¼ lbs. sliced mushrooms
- 1 tbsp. minced garlic
- 1 tbsp. Italian seasoning
- 1 (14 oz.) can chicken broth
- ½ lbs. dry linguine

- 3 cups frozen broccoli florets

Instructions:

1. Add together the first three ingredients in a bowl and set aside.
2. Heat the olive oil in the pressure cooker on the "heat" setting. Add the chicken and cook until evenly browned. Set aside.
3. Add the onion, mushrooms and peppers. Cook, stirring, for 3 minutes.
4. Add the garlic and herbs, stir and then deglaze the cooker with the broth.
5. Break the linguine noodles in half and add to the cooker. Add more water if necessary to cover the ingredients.
6. Put the chicken on top of the ingredients in the cooker. Close and lock the lid in place.
7. Set pressure cooker timer for 5 minutes.
8. Press the quick-release button and remove the lid.
9. Stir in the frozen broccoli then replace lid and set for 3 minutes more, then press the quick-release button.
10. Remove the chicken to a cutting board and stir the Alfredo sauce into cooker. Heat on the "heat" setting until heated through.
11. Serve the chicken on the linguine and broccoli.

Chicken and Mushrooms

Servings: 4

Ingredients:

- 4 boneless chicken breasts, sliced
- 2 tbsp. olive oil
- 1 chopped onion
- 1 lbs. sliced mushrooms
- ½ cup white wine
- ¼ cup heavy cream
- ¼ cup grated Parmesan
- 3 tbsp. minced garlic
- 1 tbsp. Italian seasoning
- Salt and pepper to taste

Instructions:

1. Heat the olive oil in the pressure cooker on the "heat" setting. Add the chicken and cook until evenly browned. Set aside.
2. Add the onion, peppers and mushrooms. Cook, stirring, for 3 minutes.
3. Stir in the white wine and Italian seasoning. Stir until the wine has evaporated, about 2 minutes.
4. Add the chicken back to the pressure cooker.
5. Lock the lid on the pressure cooker and set timer for 7 minutes. Allow the cooker to depressurize naturally.
6. Transfer the chicken and mushrooms to a platter.
7. Stir the cream and grated Parmesan into the sauce and cook on the "heat" setting until bubbling. Stir in the chicken and mushrooms just before serving.
8. Season with salt and pepper to taste.

Braised Pork

Servings: 4 to 6

Ingredients:

- 1 (2 to 3 lbs.) pork loin roast
- 2 tbsp. olive oil
- 1 tbsp. Italian seasoning
- Salt and pepper to taste

Instructions:

1. Rub the pork with salt, pepper and Italian seasoning.
2. Heat the olive oil in the pressure cooker on the "heat" setting. Add the pork and cook until evenly browned.
3. Pour in 1 ½ cups water. Close and secure the lid.
4. Set pressure cooker timer for 25 minutes.

5. Allow the cooker to depressurize naturally (remove plug) and when pressure is released carefully remove the lid.
6. Transfer the pork to a cutting board and let rest for 5 minutes before slicing.

Sausage and Peppers

Servings: 6

Ingredients:

- 2 lbs. Italian sausage
- 2 bell peppers, sliced
- 2 chopped zucchini
- 1 chopped onion
- 1 (28 oz.) can Italian stewed tomatoes
- 1 (16 oz.) can pasta sauce
- ½ lbs. dry penne pasta
- 1 ½ tbsp. Italian seasoning
- Grated Parmesan

Instructions:

1. Remove the sausage meat from the casings and place them in the pressure cooker. Heat on the "brown" setting and cook until crumbled and browned.
2. Drain most of the fat from the cooker and stir in the garlic, onions and peppers. Cook, stirring, for 3 minutes.
3. Stir in the remaining ingredients including the sausage and add enough water to cover the ingredients.
4. Close and lock the lid and set timer for 8 minutes.
5. Manually release the pressure and carefully remove the lid.
6. Transfer the mixture to a serving plate and garnish with grated Parmesan.

Sausage Casserole

Servings: 6

Ingredients:

- 1 lbs. sweet Italian ground sausage
- 1 tbsp. olive oil
- 1 chopped onion
- 3 cups uncooked shell pasta
- 2 cups frozen vegetables
- 3 tbsp. tomato paste
- 1 (28 oz.) can chopped tomatoes in juice
- 1 ½ cups shredded mozzarella
- Salt and pepper to taste

Instructions:

1. Heat the olive oil in the pressure cooker on the "heat" setting. Add the sausage and cook until evenly browned.
2. Stir in the onions and cook for 3 minutes until softened.
3. Add the frozen vegetables, Italian seasoning, pasta, tomato paste. *Stir to combine then add enough water to cover the ingredients.*
7. *Close and lock the lid in place and set timer for 8 minutes.*
8. Release pressure manually. Remove lid.
9. Stir in the mozzarella cheese and cover until the cheese is melted. Serve hot.

Shrimp and Scallop Pasta with Lemon

Servings: 6

Ingredients:

- 8 oz. cooked fettuccini, drained
- 2 lbs. raw shrimp, peeled and deveined
- ½ lbs. small scallops
- 1 cup onion, minced
- 1 cup seafood stock
- ½ cup white wine
- 1/3 cup soy sauce
- ¼ cup hoisin sauce
- 2 tbsp. fresh lemon juice
- 2 tbsp. butter
- 1 tbsp. minced garlic
- ½ tsp. ground turmeric
- Salt and pepper to taste

- 1/3 cup grated Parmesan

Instructions:

1. Rinse the shrimp and scallops under cold water and pat dry with paper towels.
2. Add the butter in the pressure cooker on the "heat" setting. Stir in the onion and garlic and cook until softened, about 3 minutes.
3. Stir in the remaining ingredients including the seafood. Close the lid in place.
4. Set timer for 5 minutes.
5. Allow the cooker to depressurize naturally and carefully remove the lid. Strain the mixture, discarding the liquid.
6. Spoon the seafood mixture onto the cooked pasta and toss with 1/3 cup grated Parmesan. Serve hot.

Glazed Balsamic Salmon

Servings: 4

Ingredients:

- 4 (6 oz.) salmon steaks
- ½ cup dry white wine
- 1 tbsp. low-sodium soy sauce
- ½ tsp. lemon pepper seasoning
- 2 tbsp. pure maple syrup
- 2 tbsp. good balsamic vinegar

Instructions:

1. Rinse the salmon under cold water and pat dry with paper towels.
2. Add the next three ingredients in the pressure cooking, stirring to combine.

3. Add the salmon and turn to coat.
4. Close and lock the lid in place and set timer for 6 minutes.
5. Press the quick-release button and carefully remove the lid.
6. Transfer the salmon to a serving dish and set aside.
7. Combine the remaining ingredients in the pressure cooker and bring to a boil. Cook until thickened and spoon over the salmon to serve.

Lemon Garlic Steamed Clams

Servings: 4

Ingredients:

- 2 lbs. fresh soft-shell clams
- ½ cup white wine
- 2/3 cup fresh lemon juice, divided
- 1 stick butter
- 2 tsp. garlic powder

Instructions:

1. Combine 1/3 cup lemon juice with the white wine and butter in a heat-proof dish. Microwave on high for 1 minute.
2. Stir to combine then cover and chill overnight

3. Place a rack in the pressure cooker and pour in the white wine and remaining lemon juice. Stir well.
4. Rinse the clams in cool water then add them to the pressure cooker, spreading them evenly along the rack.
5. Close and lock the lid in place and set timer for 53 minutes.
6. Press the quick-release button and carefully remove the lid.
7. Remove the clams with a slotted spoon and transfer to a serving platter.
8. Reheat the butter sauce in the microwave and serve with the clams.

Pork with Red Wine Risotto

Servings: 6

Ingredients:

- 6 bone-in pork chops
- 2 tbsp. butter
- 1 cup dry Arborio rice
- 1 chopped onion
- ½ cup red wine
- 1 tbsp. minced garlic
- 1 lemon, juiced and zested
- 1 ¼ cups chicken broth
- 1/3 cup grated Parmesan

Instructions:

1. Heat the butter in the pressure cooker on the "heat" setting. Add the pork chops and cook until browned on both sides. Set aside.
2. Stir in the garlic and onion and cook until softened, about 3 minutes.
3. Add the Arborio rice and stir to coat with oil.
4. Deglaze the cooker using the red wine then stir in the lemon juice, zest and chicken broth.
5. Close and lock the lid on the pressure cooker and set the timer for 20 minutes.
6. Release the pressure using the quick-release button.
7. Transfer the pork chops to a serving plate and stir the grated Parmesan into the rice. Serve hot.

Italian Chicken and Peppers

Servings: 4 to 6

Ingredients:

- 1 tbsp. extra-virgin olive oil
- 1 lbs. chopped chicken
- 1 cup chopped onion
- 2 bell peppers, chopped
- 2 cloves garlic, sliced
- 1 (16 oz.) can diced tomatoes
- 2 tbsp. red wine vinegar
- 1 tsp. dried basil
- Salt and pepper to taste

Instructions:

1. Pour the oil into the pressure cooker and turn it to the "heat" setting.

2. Add the chicken and cook until browned, stirring occasionally.
3. Remove the chicken and stir in the onion, pepper and garlic. Cook until the vegetables begin to soften, about 5 minutes.
4. Pour in the vinegar and stir to deglaze the bottom of the cooker.
5. Return the chicken to the cooker and stir in the remaining ingredients. Season with salt and pepper to taste.
6. Close and lock the lid on the pressure cooker and set the timer for 7 minutes.
7. Release the pressure manually and cool slightly before serving.

Carnitas

Serves: 10

Ingredients:

- 2 ½ lb. pork shoulder, chopped into ¾'' cubes
- 1 tsp. dried chipotle powder
- ½ tsp. ground cumin
- 1 large onion, coarsely chopped
- 2 cups low sodium chicken broth

To serve:

- 10 wheat tortillas, toasted
- Pico de Gallo
- Guacamole
- Shredded parmesan cheese

Method:

- Place all the ingredients into your pressure cooker and give it a nice stir to mix well.
- Set timer for about 30 minutes.
- Release the pressure naturally.
- Drain the meat out into a plate and reserve the cooking liquid.
- Shred the meat with the help of two forks and mash the onions lightly with a potato masher.
- Scatter the shredded meat across a shallow, roasting pan and broil in your oven for about 10-12 minutes, agitating it from time to time and adding splashes of reserved liquid to prevent it from drying up.
- Once the meat turns slightly crispy, remove from the oven and spoon small portions of it into the each tortilla.
- Top it up with Pico de Gallo, guacamole as well as shredded cheese and arrange them on a large serving platter.
- Serve right away.

Pork chop suey

Serves: 4

Ingredients:

- 4 pork steaks, cubed
- 6 fresh white mushrooms, roughly chopped
- 2 celery stalks, thinly sliced diagonally
- 9 oz can bean sprouts
- 2/3 yellow onion, sliced
- ¼ cup soy sauce
- 2 tbsp molasses
- 9 oz canned chicken broth
- 1 1/3 tbsp butter
- 2/3 tbsp vegetable oil
- 1 1/3 tbsp cornstarch
- 1/3 cup water
- Salt and white pepper to taste

Method:

- Set to heat. Melt butter in a pressure cooker and add the diced pork once it starts bubbling.
- Stir the pork for a couple of minutes and throw in the celery, mushrooms and onions, once the meat catches a brownish tint.
- Season with a dash of white pepper and sauté, until the veggies soften.
- Empty the cans of broth and bean sprouts into the cooker along with a splash of soy sauce and stir them all together.
- Stir in the molasses and fasten the lid into the cooker.
- Set timer for 6 minutes.
- Unplug the pressure cooker from heat and let the pressure release naturally.
- Uncover, plug back in and turn on heat setting and simmer the mixture further for another 10 minutes.
- Dissolve the cornstarch in water until the mixture is free of lumps and pour it over the mixture.
- Give it a nice stir and simmer the mixture in the heat mode for about 5 minutes or until it thickens.
- Serve right away over a bed of steamed white rice and enjoy!

Red beans and sausage

Serves: 8

Ingredients:

- 1 lb. smoked sausage, sliced
- 1 lb. red beans, dried
- ½ onion, chopped
- ½ green bell pepper, chopped
- ½ garlic clove, chopped
- 1 celery stalk, chopped
- 5 cups cold water, plus more if necessary
- 1 bay leaf
- 1 tsp. dried parsley
- 2 tbs.p Cajun seasoning
- 1 tsp. salt
- ¼ tsp. ground cumin

Method:

- Dump the sausage, red beans and veggies into a pressure cooker.

116

- Sprinkle the dried parsley, Cajun seasoning, ground cumin and salt over them and empty 5 cups of water into the cooker until the ingredients are completely immersed in it.
- Give it a good stir to mix well and secure the lid on top.
- Set timer for 20 minutes.
- Release the pressure manually and open the lid.
- Stir everything all together once more and spoon out into a large bowl.
- Serve hot.

Corned beef and cabbage

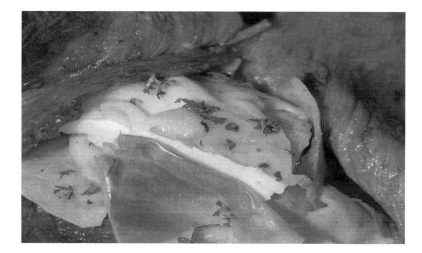

Serves: 6

Ingredients:

- 2 ½ lb point cut corned beef brisket
- 1 head cabbage, cut into 6 chunks
- 3 garlic cloves, quartered
- 3 turnips, peeled and quartered
- 6 potatoes, peeled and quartered
- 4 carrots, diced
- 2 bay leaves
- 4 cups water

Method:

- Empty the cups of water into the cooker and drop the meat into it.
- Set in heat mode and Boil the brisket and skim off the residue floating on the surface.

118

- Stir in the garlic, drop the bay leaves into it and cover the cooker with its lid.
- Set timer for 60 minutes. Release pressure naturally.
- Remove the lid to stir in the veggies and secure the lid again.
- Set timer for another 5 minutes. Release pressure naturally.
- Unfasten the lid, remove and slice the brisket and serve with the cabbage and veggies.

Homemade bread

Makes: 1 loaf

Ingredients:

- 4 cups all-purpose flour
- 1 ¾ cups water
- 1 tbsp. salt
- 2 packets yeast
- 3 tbsp. white sugar
- 3 tbsp. olive oil
- Oatmeal, as required

Method:

- Stir the sugar and salt in hot water until they dissolve and stir in the yeast.
- Let it rest for about 10 minutes to allow the yeast to become active.
- Drizzle 3 tbsp. olive oil into it and stir it into the mixture.

- Place the flour in a large mixing bowl and pour in the above mixture while stirring it into the dough at the same time.
- Work them together until they clump together to form a smooth but non-sticky dough.
- Place it on a lightly-floured working counter and knead it for several minutes or until it becomes more pliable and soft.
- Wrap it up with a moist towel and set aside for an hour in a warm, dry place, until it rises to double its volume.
- Remove the towel and knead the dough again to deflate it.

Drizzle a good lug of olive oil into 6 quart pressure cooker to grease its base and sprinkle oatmeal

Electric Pressure Cooker Snacks and Sides

<u>Included in this Section:</u>

Risotto

Slider Meatballs

Roasted Garlic Tomato Sauce

Pressure Cooked Risotto

e Meat Sauce Bolognese

Italian Sausage Red Sauce

Risotto with Wild Mushroom

Meat Sauce

Chicken Caesar-Style Rice

Risotto with Walnuts

Buttery Red Potatoes

Risotto Tomato Mozzarella

Italian Roasted Vegetables

Easy Italian Garden Rice

Brussels Sprouts in Parmesan Sauce

Italian Stewed Tomatoes

Spinach and artichoke dip

Hummus

Bolognese sauce

Ratatouille

Green bean and potato casserole

Indian style kidney beans (rajma)

Coca-cola chicken wings

Risotto

Serves: 6

Ingredients:

- 1 ½ cup Arborio rice
- 3 tbsp. parmesan cheese
- 3 ½ cup chicken stock
- 1 onion, finely chopped
- 2 tbsp. olive oil
- Black pepper for taste

Method:

- Drizzle some oil in the pressure cooker and heat it using the heat function.

- Throw in the onion and brown until it soften and turn translucent.
- Stir in the rice, pour the stock over it and secure lid.
- Set the timer to 10 minutes. (In rice mode if possible)
- Release pressure naturally. Open lid.
- Sprinkle a dash of black pepper over the risotto and top it up with cheese.
- Stir them all together and spoon it into serving plates.
- Serve right away.

Slider Meatballs

Servings: 6 to 8

Ingredients:

- 1 tbsp. butter
- 40 frozen meatballs
- 2 (16 oz.) jars marinara sauce
- 1 cup chicken broth
- ¼ cup fresh chopped basil

Instructions:

1. Melt the butter in the pressure cooker on the "heat or brown" setting.
2. Add the meatballs and stir to brown. Cook for 2 minutes, stirring often.

126

3. Pour the sauce in and mix well. Dilute with 1 cup chicken broth, if needed.
4. Close and lock the lid on the pressure cooker.
5. Set timer for 20 minutes. Release the pressure manually and open lid to stir the meatballs.
6. Let stand for 5 minutes then stir in the basil and serve hot.

Roasted Garlic Tomato Sauce

Servings: 4 to 6

Ingredients:

- 1 tbsp. olive oil
- 1 (28 oz.) can crushed tomatoes
- 3 cloves garlic
- 1 small onion, chopped
- 1 carrot, chopped
- 1 tsp. dried basil
- ½ tsp. dried oregano
- Salt and pepper to taste

Instructions:

1. Heat the olive oil in the pressure cooker on the "heat or brown" setting. Stir in the onion and garlic and cook for 1 minute.
2. Add the spices and carrots (except the salt) and stir to combine.
3. Pour in the crushed tomatoes and about a cup of water to thin out the mixture.
4. Close and lock the lid on the pressure cooker. Set timer for 20 minutes.
5. Quick-release pressure and remove the lid.
6. Season the sauce to taste and serve hot.

Creamy Risotto

Servings: 4 to 6

Ingredients:

- 2 cups dry Arborio rice
- 4 cups chicken stock
- 1 cup chopped onion
- 2 tbsp. dry white wine
- Salt and pepper to taste
- Extra-virgin olive oil

Instructions:

1. Combine the onion, salt and pepper in the pressure cooker. Drizzle with olive oil and stir to coat.
2. Turn the pressure cooker on to the "brown or heat" setting and cook, stirring, until the onions are softened.

3. Add the rice and cook, stirring, for 1 minute.
4. Stir in the white wine and cook until the liquid has evaporated.
5. Add the broth and stir then quickly place the lid on the pressure cooker.
6. Close and lock the lid on the pressure cooker and Set timer to 7 minutes.
7. Release pressure on the pressure cooker and remove the lid.
8. Stir the risotto and serve hot.

Meat Sauce Bolognese

Servings: 6

Ingredients:

- 1 lbs. ground Italian sausage
- 1 lbs. lean ground beef
- ½ lbs. ground pork
- 1 diced onion
- 1 grated carrot
- 2 tbsp. minced garlic
- 2 (28 oz.) cans chopped tomatoes
- 1 (28 oz.) can crushed tomatoes
- 1 (14 oz.) can chicken broth
- ½ cup red wine
- 1 tbsp. Italian seasoning
- Salt and pepper to taste
- ¼ cup heavy cream

132

Instructions:

1. Set the pressure cooker on heat mode and add olive oil in the pressure cooker. When hot add meat till browned.
2. Remove the meat with a slotted spoon and set on paper towels to drain. Drain all but 1 tbsp. fat from the cooker.
3. Stir in the garlic and onion and cook for 1 minute, stirring.
4. Deglaze the cooker with the wine. Add the Italian seasoning.
5. Stir in the cooked meat and the remaining ingredients (not the heavy cream).
6. Close and lock the lid on the pressure cooker and set timer for 8 minutes
7. Allow the cooker to depressurize naturally (unplug) and carefully remove the lid.
8. Stir in the heavy cream and serve hot.

Italian Sausage Red Sauce

Servings: 6

Ingredients:

- ½ lbs. ground hot Italian sausage
- 1 tbsp. olive oil
- 1 (28 oz.) can crushed tomatoes
- 2 cloves garlic, sliced
- 1 onion, chopped
- 1 carrot, chopped
- 1 tsp. dried basil
- ½ tsp. dried oregano
- Salt and pepper to taste

Instructions:

1. Heat the olive oil in the pressure cooker on the "heat" setting. Add the sausage and cook until browned. Spoon out the extra fat.
2. Stir in the garlic and onion and cook for 1 minute, stirring.
3. Add the spices and carrots and stir to combine.
4. Pour in the crushed tomatoes and a cup of water and stir.
5. Close and lock the lid on the pressure cooker and set timer for 15 minutes.
6. Release pressure naturally and remove the lid.
7. Season the sauce to taste and serve hot.

Risotto with Wild Mushroom

Servings: 4 to 6

Ingredients:

- 2 cups dry Arborio rice
- 4 cups warm water
- 2 cups sliced mushrooms
- 1 cup chopped onion
- 2 tbsp. dry white wine
- 1 package dried porcini mushrooms
- Salt and pepper to taste
- Extra-virgin olive oil

Instructions:

1. Soak the dried porcini mushrooms in 2 cups warm water for 1/2 hour.

2. Mix the onion, mushrooms, salt and pepper in the pressure cooker. Drizzle with olive oil and stir to coat.
3. Turn the pressure cooker on to the "brown" setting and cook, stirring, until the onions are softened.
4. Add the rice and cook, stirring, for 1 minute.
5. Add in the white wine and cook until the liquid has evaporated.
6. Close and lock the lid on the pressure cooker and set timer for 7 minutes.
7. Release the pressure naturally and remove the lid.
8. Stir the risotto and serve hot.

Meat Sauce

Servings: 6 to 8

Ingredients:

- 1 tbsp. olive oil
- 1 lbs. lean ground beef
- 1 cup chopped onion
- ¼ cup chopped carrot
- ¼ cup chopped celery
- 1 clove garlic, sliced
- 1 (15 oz.) can diced tomatoes
- 1 (6 oz.) can tomato paste
- ¼ cup dry white wine
- ¼ cup water
- 1 tsp. dried basil
- ½ tsp. kosher salt

Instructions:

1. Pour the olive oil into the pressure cooker and heat on the "heat" setting.
2. Add the ground beef to hot oil and cook until browned, about 5 minutes. Spoon the cooked beef into a bowl.
3. Add the vegetables, dried basil and garlic and stir. Cook on the "heat" setting for 2 to 3 minutes until softened.
4. Pour in the wine and cook for 2 minutes until the liquid is reduced.
5. Add the remaining ingredients and stir to combine. Mix in the cooked beef.
6. Close and lock the lid on the pressure cooker.
7. Set timer for 20 minutes. Release the pressure naturally and remove the lid once it has de-pressurized.
8. Season with salt as needed and serve hot.

Chicken Caesar-Style Rice

Servings: 6

Ingredients:

- 4 boneless chicken breasts
- 2 tbsp. olive oil
- 3 cups frozen mixed vegetables
- 1 cup dry long-grain rice
- 1 (14 oz.) can chicken broth
- ½ cup Caesar salad dressing
- 1 tbsp. minced garlic
- 2 tsp. Italian seasoning
- ½ cup fresh grated Parmesan

Instructions:

1. Heat the olive oil in the pressure cooker on the "heat or brown" setting. Add the chicken and cook until evenly browned.
2. Remove the chicken to a cutting board and finely chop.
3. Add the rice to the pressure cooker and stir well.
4. add the remaining ingredients and stir well (except the grated Parmesan and frozen vegetables).
5. Place the lid on the pressure cooker and lock in place.
6. Set timer for 4 minutes. Press the quick-release button and remove the lid.
7. Stir in the frozen vegetables and replace the lid. Set timer for 2 minutes.
8. Allow the cooker to depressurize naturally then remove the lid.
9. Stir in the grated Parmesan and serve hot.

Risotto with Walnuts

Servings: 4

Ingredients:

- 1/3 cup walnut halves
- 1 cup dry Arborio rice
- 2 tbsp. butter
- ½ cup chopped onion
- ½ cup white wine
- 2 tsp. minced garlic
- Salt and pepper to taste
- 3 cups chicken broth
- ¼ cup grated Parmesan

Instructions:

1. Cook the walnut halves in a heavy skillet and over medium heat for 1 to 2 minutes, stirring, until lightly toasted. Set aside to cool then chop coarsely.
2. Melt the butter in the pressure cooker on the "heat or brown" setting.
3. Stir in the garlic and onions and cook for 2 minutes.
4. Stir in the rice and stir to coat with oil. Stir in the remaining ingredients aside from the Parmesan.
5. Close and lock the lid in place and set timer for 7 minutes.
6. Manually release pressure and remove the lid carefully.
7. Stir the parmesan into the risotto and sprinkle with toasted walnuts to serve.

Buttery Red Potatoes

Servings: 4

Ingredients:

- 8 red potatoes
- 3 tbsp. butter
- 1 tbsp. minced garlic
- Salt and pepper to taste
- Fresh chopped parsley

Instructions:

1. Put a rack in the pressure cooker and pour in ½ cup water.
2. Add the potatoes to the pressure cooker.
3. Close and lock the lid in place and set timer for 8 minutes.
4. Allow the cooker to depressurize naturally and remove the lid carefully.

144

5. Remove the potatoes to a cutting board and slice thick. Place them in a large bowl and top with the garlic and butter.

6. When the butter melts toss to combine. Season with salt and pepper to taste and toss with fresh chopped parsley to serve.

Risotto Tomato Mozzarella

Servings: 3 to 4

Ingredients:

- 1 tbsp. olive oil
- 1 ½ cups Arborio rice
- 1 (15 oz.) can diced tomatoes
- 1 cup diced onion
- ½ cup dry white wine
- ½ cup sliced green olives
- 2 tsp. Italian seasoning
- 2 ½ cups vegetable broth
- 1 cup shredded mozzarella
- 1 cup chopped parsley
- Salt and pepper to taste

Instructions:

1. Combine the olive oil, onion and Italian seasoning in the pressure cooker on the "heat or brown" setting. Cook for 1 minute.
2. Add the Arborio rice and white wine. Add the tomato, vegetable broth and olives and stir well.
3. Close and lock the lid in place.
4. Set timer for 5 minutes.
5. Release the pressure quickly by pressing the quick-release button.
6. Remove the lid and set to the "heat" setting. Cook the risotto, stirring constantly, for 3 to 4 minutes until creamy.
7. Stir in the mozzarella and parsley. Season with salt to taste.
8. Stir for 5-10 minutes until the cheese has just melted. Serve hot.

Italian Roasted Vegetables

Servings: 6

Ingredients:

- 1 lbs. Brussels sprouts, trimmed
- 1 lbs. Swiss chard, chopped
- 1 head cauliflower, chopped
- 1 zucchini, sliced
- 1 onion, sliced
- 1 cup chopped celery
- 1 cup chopped carrot
- 4 tbsp. butter, melted
- 1 tbsp. minced garlic
- ½ cup grated Parmesan
- ¼ cup heavy cream

Instructions:

1. Stir together the butter, garlic, grated Parmesan and heavy cream in a small heat proof bowl. Set aside.
2. Place a rack in the pressure cooker and pour in 1 cup water.
3. Add all of the vegetables to the pressure cooker. Lock the lid in place and set timer for 7 minutes.
4. Use the quick-release method and remove the lid carefully.
5. Drain the vegetables and transfer to a serving platter.

Heat the sauce in the microwave until warm then pour over the vegetables to serve.

Easy Italian Garden Rice

Servings: 6

Ingredients:

- 1 cup dry long-grain rice
- 3 tbsp. butter
- 3 cups frozen mixed vegetables
- 1 chopped red onion
- ¼ cup fresh lemon juice
- 1 (14 oz.) can vegetable broth
- 2 tsp. ground cumin
- Salt and pepper to taste

Instructions:

1. Heat the butter in the pressure cooker on the "heat or brown" setting and mix in the onion and garlic. Cook for 2 minutes until soft.
2. Add the rice and stir to coat with butter.
3. Stir in the remaining ingredients.
4. Close and lock the lid on the pressure cooker and set timer for 4 minutes.
5. Allow the cooker to depressurize naturally and remove the lid.
6. Stir the mixture to fluff the rice then transfer to a bowl to serve.

Brussels Sprouts in Parmesan Sauce

Servings: 4

Ingredients:

- 1 lbs. Brussels sprouts, trimmed
- 2 tbsp. butter
- ¼ cup onion, minced
- ¼ cup orange juice
- ¼ cup grated Parmesan
- 1 tbsp. soy sauce
- 2 tsp. minced garlic
- Pinch ground pepper

Instructions:

1. Heat the butter in the pressure cooker on the "heat or brown" setting and stir in the onion and garlic. Cook for 2 minutes until soft.
2. Add in the remaining ingredients aside from the parmesan and stir to combine.
3. Lock the lid in place set the timer for 5 minutes.
4. Allow the cooker to depressurize naturally and remove the lid.
5. Scoop the Brussels sprouts out with a slotted spoon and heat the sauce in the pressure cooker on the "heat" setting.
6. Stir in the grated Parmesan and return the Brussels sprouts to the cooker. Toss to coat and cook until heated through.

Italian Stewed Tomatoes

Servings: 4

Ingredients:

- 8 Roma tomatoes, peeled and cored
- 2 tbsp. olive oil
- 2 stalks celery, sliced thin
- 1 diced onion
- ½ green pepper, diced
- 3 tbsp. sugar
- ½ tsp. dried oregano
- 1 tsp. salt
- ½ tsp. black pepper

154

Instructions:

1. Heat the olive oil in the pressure cooker on the "heat or brown" setting and stir in the pepper, onion, celery and garlic. Cook for 2 minutes until soft.
2. Slice the tomatoes and add them to the pressure cooker along with the juice.
3. Stir in the remaining ingredients and add ½ cup water.
4. Close and lock the lid in place and set timer for 5 minutes.
5. Use the quick-release option and remove the lid. Season the tomatoes to taste.

Spinach and artichoke dip

Serves: 4-5

Ingredients:

- 1 can (14 oz.) artichoke hearts, drained and roughly chopped
- 1 package (10 oz.) frozen spinach, thawed, drained and chopped
- ½ cup sour cream
- 1 cup mozzarella cheese, shredded
- 1 cup Parmesan cheese, grated
- 1 cup light mayonnaise
- ½ cup sour cream
- Pinch of cayenne pepper
- ¼ tsp. garlic salt

Method:

- Put all its ingredients together in a large bowl and stir them all together until well combined.

156

- Pour it into a 1-quart baking pan and spread it evenly throughout it.
- Spread a heavy-duty aluminum foil on top of the dish to cover.
- Place a wire rack in the pressure cooker.
- Fold an 18'' foil strip twice to create a foil sling and place it on a wire rack.
- Position the rack within the cooker and place the baking dish on top of the foil strip.
- Secure lid and set timer for 10 minutes then release pressure and open lid.
- Remove the pan carefully from the cooker, using the foil sling and serve warm alongside tortilla chips or French bread slices.

Hummus

Makes: 2 cups

Ingredients:

- 1 cup chickpeas
- 2 tbsp. fresh lemon juice
- 1 garlic clove, peeled and minced
- 1 tsp. dried parsley
- 2 tbsp. tahini salt
- 4 cups water
- ¼ cup extra virgin olive oil
- 2 tsp. vegetable oil

Method:

- Empty the cups of chickpeas and water into a pressure cooker and drizzle the oil into it.
- Secure the lid and set timer for 25 minutes.
- Turn off the heat and let pressure release naturally.

- Open the lid and drain them out into a colander.
- Pour them into a food processor, along with rest of the ingredients, except olive oil, and blitz them into a smooth puree.
- Drizzle the olive oil into it, while the processor is still running and pulse the puree further until well combined with the oil.
- Scoop it out into a serving bowl and serve alongside toasted pita chips.

Bolognese sauce

Serves: 4-6

Ingredients:

- 11 oz. ground beef
- 1 celery stalks, chopped
- 1 carrot, chopped
- 1 white onion, chopped
- 4 oz. unsmoked bacon, diced
- 5 tbsp. tomato paste
- 1 tbsp. cream
- 1 cup beef stock
- ½ cup dry red wine
- Salt and freshly ground black pepper to taste

Method:

- Set the pressure cooker in heat mode. Toss the diced bacon into a pressure cooker for about 5 minutes or until the fat is rendered and the bacon sizzles.
- Stir in the celery, carrot as well as onions and sauté until they soften.
- Dump the ground beef into it and brown, stirring often, until the meat dries up and the fat sizzles,
- Add a splash of wine and cook until the alcohol ebbs away.
- Whisk the tomato paste and a dash of seasonings into the beef stock and pour it into the cooker.
- Stir all together and lock the lid to secure.
- Set timer for 10 minutes
- Release pressure manually.
- Open the cooker.
- Give it a nice stir to mix well.
- Pour the sauce into a serving bowl.
- Whisk in the cream until well combined and serve right away.

Ratatouille

Serves: 6

Ingredients:

- 1 small eggplant, peeled and diced
- 1 potato, diced
- 2 tomatoes, chopped
- 2 green peppers, seeded and longitudinally sliced
- 2 zucchini, thinly sliced
- 2 garlic cloves, minced
- 1 large onion, chopped
- 2 tbsp. parsley, minced
- 4 tbsp. olive oil
- ¼ cup chicken stock

Method:

- Pour 2 tbsp. oil in a pressure cooker and add the potato, zucchini, eggplant and peppers once it heats up. (heat mode)

162

- Sauté the veggies briskly, in batches if needed, and transfer them to a plate.
- Drizzle the remaining oil into the cooker and throw in the onions as well as garlic to sauté them until the former softens.
- Add the veggies back into the cooker and the rest of the ingredients before locking the lid.
- Set timer for 10 minutes.
- Let go of the pressure swiftly by automated or quick release method and open the lid.
- Simmer the stew for a couple of minutes, uncovered and pour it into a large serving bowl.

Green bean and potato casserole

Serves: 4

Ingredients:

- ¾ lb. green beans
- 3 potatoes, peeled and cubed
- 1 green pepper, diced
- A garlic clove, minced
- 1 onion, minced
- 1 tbsp. minced parsley
- ½ cup chicken stock
- 1 tbsp. olive oil
- ½ cup chicken stock

Method:

- Add all the ingredients into a pressure cooker and toss them well to mix.
- Set the timer for 4 minutes.
- Release the pressure quickly and remove the lid.
- Pour the casserole into a serving bowl and enjoy this easy and sumptuous dish with utmost delight.

Indian style kidney beans (rajma)

Serves: 6

Ingredients:

- 1 lb. red kidney beans, soaked overnight
- 1 onion, finely chopped
- 2 garlic cloves, minced
- 2 '' fresh ginger, minced
- 3 tomatoes, chopped
- 2 tsp. plain yogurt
- ¼ tsp. asafetida
- 2 tsp. garam masala powder
- ¼ tsp. turmeric powder
- ½ tsp. red chili powder
- 1 tsp. cumin seeds
- 2 tsp. ground coriander seeds
- 2 sprigs coriander leaves, finely chopped
- 3 tsp. vegetable oil
- Salt to taste

166

Method:

- Add the beans to a pressure cooker and sprinkle turmeric as well as salt over them.
- Set the timer for 15 minutes.
- Meanwhile, sauté the onions and tomatoes in oil along with garlic, ginger and cumin seeds.
- Release the pressure naturally and open the lid to add the sautéed mixture into the cooker.
- Sprinkle the spices over them and simmer, in heat mode uncovered, for a couple of minutes.
- Stir in the yogurt and cook for about 5 minutes until it begins to boil.
- Stir in the coriander leaves and serve hot.

Coca-cola chicken wings

Ingredients:

- 2 lbs. chicken wings
- 2 cup coca-cola
- 2 tbsp. chinese cooking wine
- ¼ cup soy sauce
- 2 tbsp. green onions, finely chopped
- 2 tbsp. fresh garlic, finely chopped
- 2 tbsp. butter, softened
- 1 tbsp. flour
- Salt and pepper to taste

Method:

- Season the chicken wings with salt and pepper.

- Put the seasoned chicken into the pressure cooker along with the rest of the ingredients and secure lid.
- Set the timer for 15 minutes.
- Once the time is up, release pressure manually and unlock the cooker.
- Strain out the chicken into serving plates and set aside.
- Skim off half of the cooking liquid and simmer the remaining half in the cooker to half, without the lid on.
- Blend the flour and butter together into a uniform mixture and stir it into the sauce.
- Heat the sauce for about 10 minutes or until it thickens and reduces to half its volume.
- Bathe the chicken wings with the sauce and serve right away.

Electric Pressure Cooker Soups and Stews

<u>Included in this Section:</u>

Beef-noodle soup

Homemade Chicken Stock

Beef Stew Italiano

Chicken Italian Soup

Beef and Barley Soup

Chicken Lemon Rice Soup

Tomato Soup with Herbs

Butternut Squash Soup

Split pea soup

Pinto bean soup

Vegetable Soup with Ham

Cream of carrot soup

Beef stew

British Fish Stew

Chicken drumsticks and vegetables soup

Italian Beef Stew

Italian chicken stew

Beef-noodle soup

Serves: 4

Ingredients:

- 1 ½ lb. lean beef
- 6 oz. egg noodles, uncooked
- ½ Spanish onion, diced
- 1 can diced tomatoes, juice reserved
- 10 oz. baby carrots, sliced
- 2 tsp. Worcestershire sauce
- 16 oz. chicken stock
- 16 oz. beef stock
- 1 tbsp. oil, for cooking
- Salt and ground black pepper to taste

Method:

- Set pressure cooker to heat and drizzle some oil into it.

- Brown the beef in the cooker before you stir in the onions as well as carrots and stir-fry them until they soften.
- Empty the can of tomatoes into the cooker, along with its juices, followed by chicken and beef stock; stir well to mix.
- Add a splash of Worcestershire sauce into the mixture
- Sprinkle a dash of seasonings according to your liking and secure lid.
- Set timer for 30 minutes.
- Unplug the cooker and let pressure release before opening lid.
- Transfer the beef onto a plate and cut it into bite sized chunks.
- Return the beef chunks into the cooker and secure the lid.
- Plug it in set on heat and bring the soup to boil.
- Dump the egg noodles into it and cook them, leaving the cooker uncovered, until the noodles turn tender.
- Turn off the cooker.
- Spoon soup into serving soup bowls and serve.

Homemade Chicken Stock

Servings: 2 quarts

Ingredients:

- 3 lbs. chicken wings or bones
- ½ lbs. chopped carrots
- ½ lbs. chopped celery
- ½ lbs. chopped onion
- 1 tbsp. kosher salt
- ½ tsp. black peppercorns
- Water

Instructions:

1. Mix all ingredients in the pressure cooker and add enough water to cover the ingredients. Do not fill beyond the "maximum fill" line.
2. Close and lock the lid in place set timer for 20 minutes.
3. Reduce the heat to the "heat" setting and cook for 40 minutes longer.
4. Release the pressure and carefully remove the lid.
5. Strain the mixture through a mesh sieve or cheesecloth and discard the solids.
6. Chill the stock overnight then skim the fat before using.

Beef Stew Italiano

Servings: 6 to 8

Ingredients:

- 2 lbs. stew beef
- 2 tbsp. olive oil
- 2 onions, quartered
- 1 (28 oz.) can diced tomatoes
- 1 (14 oz.) can kidney beans, rinsed and drained
- 3 cups tomato-vegetable juice
- 1 ½ cups beef broth
- ½ cup red wine
- 2 tsp. dried basil
- 2 tsp. dried oregano
- 1 tsp. dried rosemary
- 2 zucchini, sliced

- 2 cups baby spinach
- Salt and pepper to taste

Instructions:

1. Heat the olive oil in the pressure cooker on the "heat" setting. Add the stew beef and cook until browned, about 3 minutes. Scoop the meat out of the cooker.
2. Stir in the onion and cook until softened, about 3 minutes.
3. Pour in the wine and cook for 1 minute, stirring, to deglaze the bottom of the cooker.
4. Return the meat to the pressure cooker and add the remaining ingredients except for the zucchini and spinach.
5. Close and lock the lid on the pressure cooker and set timer for 15 minutes.
6. Press the quick-release button and remove the lid
7. Stir in the zucchini and spinach then place the lid back on the cooker.
8. Set the cooker 2 minute.
9. Allow the cooker to depressurize naturally then remove the lid.
10. Season with salt and pepper to taste. Serve hot.

Chicken Italian Soup

Servings: 8

Ingredients:

- 1 tbsp. olive oil
- 2 boneless chicken breasts
- 1 cup chopped onion
- 1 (16 oz.) bag chopped spinach
- 1 (15 oz.) can chickpeas, drained
- 1 cup diced tomatoes
- 1 cup green lentils
- ½ cup pearl barley
- 3 cups chicken broth
- ½ cup chopped parsley leaves
- Salt and pepper to taste

Instructions:

1. Heat the olive oil in the pressure cooker on the "heat or brown" setting.
2. Stir in the onion and garlic and cook until tender, about 3 minutes.
3. Add the barley and cook for 1 minute, stirring.
4. Stir in the lentils, chicken, parsley and chicken stock. Only add enough stock to cover the ingredients in the pressure cooker.
5. Close and lock the lid on the pressure cooker set timer for 10 minutes.
6. Manually quick-release pressure and remove the lid.
7. Remove the chicken and shred it with two forks. Stir the chicken back into the soup along with the chickpeas, spinach and diced tomatoes.
8. Heat through on the "heat" setting and serve hot.

Beef and Barley Soup

Servings: 6 to 8

Ingredients:

- 2 lbs. round steak, chopped
- ½ cup all-purpose flour
- 2 tbsp. olive oil
- 1 chopped onion
- 1 cup chopped celery
- 1 cup chopped carrot
- 1 cup sliced mushrooms
- 2 (14 oz.) cans beef broth
- ½ cup dry red wine
- 1/3 cup pearl barley
- 1 tsp. dried oregano
- Salt and pepper to taste

Instructions:

1. Mix the salt, pepper and flour in a plastic bag. Add the beef and shake to coat it evenly.
2. Heat the olive oil in the pressure cooker on the "heat" setting. Add the meat and cook until evenly browned. Set aside.
3. Stir in the garlic and onions, cooking for 2 minutes or until tender.
4. Add the wine and stir to deglaze the bottom of the cooker.
5. Add in the mushrooms, barley, broth and spices and stir. Return the meat to the cooker and stir in the carrots and celery.
6. Pour in enough water to cover the ingredients by 3 inches or so.
7. Close and lock the lid on the pressure cooker and set timer for 16 minutes
8. Allow the cooker to depressurize naturally. Season to taste and serve hot.

Chicken Lemon Rice Soup

Servings: 4

Ingredients:

- 2 boneless chicken breasts
- 2 tbsp. olive oil
- ½ cup sliced celery
- ½ cup chopped carrots
- ½ cup chopped onion
- 2 tsp. minced garlic
- 2 (14 oz.) cans chicken broth
- 1/3 cup dry long-grain rice
- 1 tsp. chicken bouillon granules
- Salt and pepper to taste
- 2 tbsp. all-purpose flour
- ¼ cup fresh lemon juice

Instructions:

1. Heat the olive oil in the pressure cooker on the "heat" setting. Add the chicken and cook until evenly browned.
2. Transfer the chicken to a cutting board and chop it finely. Set aside.
3. Add in the celery, onions and garlic and stir, cooking for 2 minutes or until tender.
4. Add the carrots, rice, chicken broth and bouillon granules.
5. Close and lock the lid on the pressure cooker and set timer for 10 minutes.
6. Allow the cooker to depressurize naturally.
7. Whisk together the 2 tbsp. all-purpose flour and ¼ cup lemon juice to form a slurry. Set aside.
Remove the lid and stir in the lemon juice mixture. Heat on the "brown" setting until slightly thickened. Serve hot.

Tomato Soup with Herbs

Servings: 6

Ingredients:

- 8 large tomatoes, chopped
- ¼ cup butter
- 2 stalks celery, chopped
- 1 grated carrot
- 1 chopped onion
- 1 tbsp. minced garlic
- 3 (14 oz.) cans chicken or vegetable broth
- ½ cup chopped cilantro
- 1 tbsp. Italian seasoning
- 2 bay leaves
- Salt and pepper to taste

Instructions:

1. Heat half the butter in the pressure cooker on the "heat" setting.
2. Stir in the onions, celery and garlic and cook for 3 minutes.
3. Put in the remaining ingredients plus 2 cups of water, stirring to combine.
4. Close and lock the lid on the pressure cooker and set timer for 15 **minutes**
5. Allow the cooker to depressurize naturally then remove the lid.
6. Discard the bay leaves then pour the soup into a bowl.
7. Puree the soup using an immersion blender or by blending it in batches in a food processor or blender.
8. Reheat in the pressure cooker if needed. Serve hot.

Butternut Squash Soup

Servings: 6 to 8

Ingredients:

- 4 lbs. butternut squash
- 2 red onions, chopped
- 1 cup chopped carrot
- 1 cup chopped celery
- 3 cloves garlic, sliced
- 8 cups vegetable stock
- 1 tsp. dried rosemary
- Salt and pepper to taste
- Olive oil

Instructions:

1. Cut the squash in half and remove the seeds. Chop the squash into 1-inch chunks.
2. Mix the squash, onion, carrot, celery and garlic in the pressure cooker. Drizzle with oil and toss to coat.
3. Turn the pressure cooker on to the "heat" setting and cook, stirring, for 10 minutes until the vegetables are lightly browned.
4. Add the remaining ingredients.
5. Close and lock the lid on the pressure cooker and set timer for 20 minutes.
6. Release the pressure naturally and remove the lid. Transfer the soup to a large bowl and let cool slightly.
7. Puree the soup using an immersion blender and serve hot.

Split pea soup

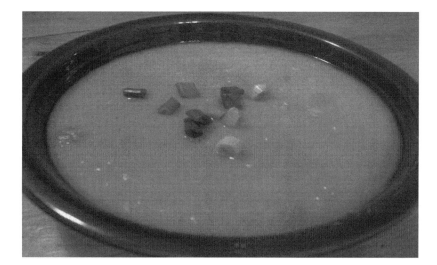

Serves: 6

Ingredients:

- 1 lb. split peas, dried
- 1 lb. ham, cut into bite-sized chunks
- 2 celery ribs, diced
- 2 carrots, diced
- 1 onion, diced
- 1 ½ tsp. dried thyme, crushed
- 8 cups water
- Sherry wine (optional)

Method:

- Dump all the ingredients, except the sherry into a pressure cooker and fasten the lid.
- Set the pressure cooker for 20 minutes.

- Release the pressure manually and open the lid.
- Sprinkle some salt over the soup to season along with a bout of sherry if you wish and give it a nice stir to mix well.
- Ladle the soup into serving soup bowls and serve hot with crusted bread or croutons.

Pinto bean soup

Serves: 4

Ingredients:

- 1 cup pinto beans, soaked overnight in cold water
- 1 ½ cups ham, diced
- 1 onion, chopped into small dices
- 1 can green Anaheim chilies, diced
- 1 can petite diced tomatoes
- ½ cup fresh cilantro, chopped
- 4 tsp. olive oil, divided
- 1 package Goya Ham flavoured concentrate
- 2 tsp. ground cumin
- 1 tbsp. dried cilantro
- Finely sliced green onions, for serving

Method:

- Drain the soaked beans out in a colander and transfer them into a pressure cooker.

190

- Empty 3 cups of water into it, followed by a lashing of half of the olive oil.
- Secure the lid and set timer for 8 minutes and then use the quick-release method to get rid of the pressure within the cooker.
- Remove the lid and drain the cooked beans out into a colander; reserve the cooking liquid.
- Clean the pressure cooker and wipe it dry with a kitchen towel.
- Place back on heat and drizzle rest of the oil into it. Put the onions in the cooker.
- Sauté for a couple of minutes, stirring often, until they soften and stir in the ground cumin, dried cilantro and green chilies.
- Stir fry them further for another couple of minutes and add the beans into it, followed by the chicken broth, flavor concentrate and the reserved liquid.
- Stir them all together to mix well and fasten the lid and set timer for 3 minutes.
- Cook likewise for about 3 minutes and then bring the pressure down by quick-release method.
- Remove the lid and fold in the fresh cilantro until they are distributed evenly throughout the soup.
- Ladle it into serving bowls and sprinkle sliced green onions on top to garnish.
- Serve hot.

Vegetable Soup with Ham

Serves:

Ingredients

1 cup white beans, soaked overnight in cold water

- 1 cup diced ham
- 1 onion, chopped into 1'' chunks
- 4 garlic cloves
- ½ cup celery, chopped
- 1 large carrot, sliced longitudinally into semi-circles
- 2 bay leaves
- Ham rinds, as required
- 3 cups water
- Chopped fresh parsley, to garnish

Method:

- Drain the white beans in a colander and pour them into your pressure cooker.
- Pour in 3 cups water and dr
- and heat the cook op in the garlic cloves as well as bay leaves.
- Secure the lid.
- Set timer for 10 minutes and allow the pressure to release using quick release method.
- Open the lid and remove the garlic as well as bay leaves.
- Toss the diced ham and chopped veggies into the cooker and scatter a small handful of ham rinds into it.
- Stir them all together and Lock lid and set timer for 2 more minutes.
- Release the pressure slowly and open the lid.
- Throw away the ham rinds and ladle the soup into serving bowls.

Cream of carrot soup

Serves: 16

Ingredients:

- 6 cups baby carrots
- 1 ½ cups celery, coarsely chopped
- 8 garlic cloves, peeled
- 6 green onions, chopped
- 1 large Yukon Gold potato, peeled and cubed
- 2 ½ cups onions, diced
- ½ tsp. mild curry powder
- Salt and freshly ground black pepper to taste
- 4 cups heavy whipping cream
- 10 cups vegetable broth
- ¼ cup butter

Method:

- Add olive oil or butter into the pressure cooker and melt it over moderate heat.
- Throw in the onions and sprinkle a dash of salt into it.
- Sauté it for about 3 minutes, or until the onion softens as well as turn lucid.
- Dump rest of the veggies, except carrots, and sauté further for another 5 minutes or until they soften slightly.
- Dump the carrots into it and pour in the vegetable broth.
- Give them a nice stir to mix well and secure the lid.
- Set timer for 7 minutes and release pressure. Open lid.
- Sprinkle the curry powder into it and stir it into the soup, along with the cream.
- Tip the contents of the cooker into an immersion blender and pulse them into a smooth puree.
- Adjust the seasonings and ladle it into soup bowls.
- Serve warm.

Beef stew

Serves: 4

Ingredients:

- 1 lb. lean beef
- 14 oz. tomatoes, juices reserved
- ½ cup onion, chopped
- 2 cups potatoes, diced
- 2 tbsp. minced garlic
- ½ cup carrot, chopped
- ¼ cup flour
- ½ cup beef broth
- 2 tbsp. balsamic vinegar
- 2 tbsp. tomato paste
- ¼ tsp. dry mustard
- 1 ½ tsp. dried thyme
- 1 tbsp. brown sugar
- 2 bay leaves
- 1 ½ tsp. olive oil

196

- Salt and pepper to taste

Method:

- Add some flour into a large zip lock along with ½ tsp. salt as well as mustard and shake the bag well to mix.
- Add the meat into the bag, seal it and shake until the beef is properly coated with the seasoned flour.
- Set to heat mode, Drizzle some oil in a pressure cooker and add the beef once it heats up.
- Cook the beef in it until it turns brown on all sides and then stir in the broth.
- Bring the mixture to boil and throw in rest of the ingredients before securing the lid.
- Set timer for 12 minutes.
- Let go of the pressure slowly (naturally) and do away with the bay leaves.
- Pour it into a large bowl and serve right away.

British Fish Stew

Serves: 4

Ingredients:

- 1 lb. white fish fillets, chopped into ½'' chunks
- 4 red potatoes, peeled and chopped into ½'' cubes
- 1 large Vidalia onion, diced
- 2 celery stalks, diced
- 1 cup frozen corn kernels, thawed
- 1 cup cold water
- 1 cup heavy cream
- 2 cups fish stock
- ½ tsp. dried thyme
- 1 bay leaf
- 2 tbsp. butter
- Salt and freshly ground black pepper to taste

Method:

- Melt the butter in the pressure cooker in heat mode until it foams and throw in the onions.
- Sauté for a couple of minutes, stirring often, until they soften and toss rest of the veggies into the cooker.
- Continue to sauté for another minute, stirring at times, and plop in the fish chunks.
- Pour in the water as well as fish stock and drop in the bay leaf.
- Sprinkle the dried thyme into it and secure the lid.
- Set the timer for 5 minutes.
- Remove from heat and allow the pressure to come down using quick-release method.
- Open the lid and remove the bay leaf.
- Set on heat mode. Add the corn and stir it into the mixture, along with the cream until well combined.
- Adjust the seasonings and bring it to a simmer, uncovered, until the corn softens and the stew is warmed through.
- Ladle it into serving bowl and add an extra dollop of butter on top of each serving.
- Serve hot.

Chicken drumsticks and vegetables soup

Serves: 6

Ingredients:

- 1 ¼ lbs. chicken drumsticks, skinned
- 1 package (10 oz.) frozen baby peas, thawed
- 1 package (10 oz.) frozen green beans, thawed
- 6 medium russet potatoes, peeled and quartered
- 1 garlic clove, peeled and minced
- 12 pearl onions, peeled
- 6 carrots, peeled and sliced
- 2 celery stalks, finely diced
- 2 cans (15 oz. each) diced tomatoes
- 1 package (10 oz.) frozen kernel corn, thawed
- ½ oz. dried mushrooms
- 2 orange zest strips
- 1 bay leaf
- ¼ tsp. dried rosemary
- ¼ tsp. dried oregano

200

- Salt and freshly ground black pepper to taste
- 1 tbsp. extra-virgin olive oil
- Fresh chopped parsley leaves, for serving

Method:

- Heat the oil in a pressure cooker in heat mode and add the garlic into it.
- Sauté briskly for about 10 seconds, stirring constantly and empty the can of tomatoes into it.
- Dump rest of the veggies, mushrooms as well as orange zest and drop in the bay leaf.
- Sprinkle the dried herbs as well as a dash of seasonings over them and stir them all together until well combined.
- Arrange the chicken drumsticks on top, with the flesh-side facing down and secure the lid.
- Set timer for 10 minutes.
- Allow the pressure to release naturally.
- Open the cooker and transfer the drumsticks onto chopping board.
- Chop it into bite-sized chunks and dump it back into the cooker. Turn to heat.
- Stir in the thawed ingredients and simmer, uncovered, for about 5 minutes over moderate heat, until heated
- Ladle the soup into serving bowls and sprinkle the chopped parsley on top.
- Serve hot.

Italian Beef Stew

Servings: 6 to 8

Ingredients:

- 2 lbs. stew beef
- 2 tbsp. olive oil
- 2 onions, quartered
- 1 (28 oz.) can diced tomatoes
- 1 (14 oz.) can kidney beans, rinsed and drained
- 3 cups tomato-vegetable juice
- 1 ½ cups beef broth
- ½ cup red wine
- 2 tsp. dried basil
- 2 tsp. dried oregano
- 1 tsp. dried rosemary
- 2 zucchini, sliced

- 2 cups baby spinach
- Salt and pepper to taste

Instructions:

1. Heat the olive oil in the pressure cooker on the "heat" setting. Add the stew beef and cook until browned, about 3 minutes. Scoop the meat out of the cooker.
2. Stir in the onion and cook until softened, about 3 minutes.
3. Pour in the wine and cook for 1 minute, stirring, to deglaze the bottom of the cooker.
4. Return the meat to the pressure cooker and add the remaining ingredients except for the zucchini and spinach.
5. Close and lock the lid on the pressure cooker and set timer for 12 minutes.
6. Press the quick-release button and remove the lid
7. Stir in the zucchini and spinach then place the lid back on the cooker.
8. Set the cooker 2 minute.
9. Allow the cooker to depressurize naturally then remove the lid.
10. Season with salt and pepper to taste. Serve hot.

Italian chicken stew

Ingredients:

- 2 lbs. chicken breasts
- 2 garlic cloves, finely chopped
- 1 medium onion, roughly chopped
- 1 14 oz. can tomatoes
- 1 cup bell pepper, chopped
- 1 cup celery, chopped
- 1 cup frozen squash
- 1 tsp. dried basil
- 1 tsp. Italian seasoning
- 2 bay leaves
- 1 tsp. oregano
- Juice of a lemon

Method:

- Add the chicken into the pressure cooker, along with the tomatoes, garlic and rest of the veggies, except the squash.
- Pour a cup of water over them and sprinkle the seasonings one by one.
- Stir them well to mix and put the lid on the cooker.
- Set the timer to 25 minutes.
- Once the time is up, allow the pressure to drop down and open the lid.
- Stir in the frozen squash and keep the stew warm inside the cooker for 5-10 minutes.
- Serve over a bed of rice or pasta.

Electric Pressure Cooker Desserts

Plum pudding

Serves: 10

Ingredients:

- 1 ½ cups all-purpose flour
- 1 cup dried breadcrumbs
- ½ tsp. salt
- 1 tsp. baking soda
- 1 cup butter, softened
- 2 cups light brown sugar, packed
- 3 eggs
- ½ cup dark rum
- 1 tbsp. candied ginger, minced

- 1 cup candied lemon peel, minced
- 1 cup raisins
- 1 cups prunes, snipped
- ½ cup pecans, chopped
- 1 cup dried cranberries
- 1 cup dried currants
- ¼ tsp. ground cloves
- ¼ tsp. ground nutmeg
- 1 tsp. ground cinnamon
- ¼ cup brandy
- 1 cup heavy cream
- 3 cups water

Method:

- Pour the dark rum in a bowl and soak the candied lemon peel and dried fruits in it, covered, for about 8 hours.
- Place the flour in a large mixing bowl and stir in the breadcrumbs, baking soda, candied ginger, ground spices and a dash of salt until well combined.
- Grate the butter into it and drain the soaked fruits into it.
- Stir them into the dry mixture and set aside.
- Crack the eggs into a separate bowl and whisk them thoroughly, along with a cup of brown sugar until they blend thoroughly into a uniform, pale mixture.
- Pour it into the dry mixture and fold them together until they are blended thoroughly into a uniform batter.
- Spread a sheet of aluminum foil across the base of a 8'' springform pan and pour the batter into it.
- Get rid of any trapped air by pressing it down with a spatula and cover the surface of the pan with a pre-greased 25'' long aluminum foil, while tucking its overhanging portion under and over the base of the pan.
- Position a rack within your pressure cooker and pour in water until it reaches ¾ of the rack.
- Create handles along either edges of the rack, using double strips of foil
- Add a cup of brown sugar and place the cake pan on top.

207

- Secure the lid and set timer for 45 minutes.
- Set the cooker aside until the pressure comes down naturally and unlock the lid.
- Transfer the cake pan onto a wire rack, outside the cooker and peel off the top foil.
- Set aside for about 15 minutes to cool and loosen up its sides by running a sharp knife along its edges.
- Invert it onto a plate and allow to cool completely.
- To make the brandy sauce, dump rest of the ingredients, except brandy, into a saucepan and cook it over moderately high heat until it begins to simmer.
- Continue to simmer, while stirring relentlessly until the sugar dissolves completely and add a splash of brandy into it.
- Continue to simmer for another 10 minutes, while stirring often and drizzle it over the plum pudding.
- Slice and serve.

Coconut custard

Serves: 8

Ingredients:

- 1 can (14 oz) coconut milk
- 2 cups water
- 1 cup whole milk
- 1 can (10 oz.) condensed milk, sweetened
- 3 egg yolks
- 3 eggs
- ½ tsp. pure vanilla extract

Method:

- Pour in all types of specified milk into a saucepan and heat it over high flame until starts boiling gently.
- Whisk in a splash of vanilla and continue to simmer over slightly-reduced heat.

209

- Crack the eggs in a separate bowl and whisk them together along with egg yolks until well combined into a pale mixture.
- Spoon in 2 tbsp. of the warm milk into the whisked eggs and beat them together until well combined.
- Tip the above mixture back into the simmering milk and give it a nice stir to mix well.
- Continue to simmer over slow heat for about 4 minutes, stirring regularly, until the mixture turns thicker.
- Grease a 6-cup soufflé pan with a lashing of oil or butter and spoon the heated mixture into each cup, leaving ¼ of it empty.
- Place an aluminum foil on top of the soufflé dish and fold the sides under the pan to seal.
- Position a wire rack within the cooker and place the soufflé dish on top.
- Fill it up with water until it reaches ¾ of the wire rack and lock the lid.
- Set timer for 30 minutes.
- Allow the pressure to come down slowly.
- Unlock the lid and remove the pan from the cooker.
- Allow to cool on another wire rack, outside the cooker and peel off the foil.
- Pat the surface of the custard with paper towel to get rid of any excess moisture and leave in the fridge until the time of serving.
- Slice and serve chilled.

Blueberry jam

Makes: 4 cups

Ingredients:

- 4 cups fresh blueberries
- 1 package (1 ¾ oz.) dry pectin
- 1 cup orange juice
- 4 cups granulated cane sugar
- 1 tsp. orange zest, finely grated
- Pinch of salt
- Pinch of ground nutmeg

Method:

- Toss the blueberries into a pressure cooker and pour in the orange juice.

- Empty the cups of sugar into it, followed by orange zest, a dash of salt as well as ground nutmeg and give them a good stir to mix well.
- Secure the lid and set timer for 3 minutes.
- Reduce pressure naturally and unlock the lid.
- Tip the contents of the cooker into a strainer and press thee blueberries with a spatula to strain out the pulp into a bowl; get rid of the solids.
- Pour the pulp back into the cooker on heat mode, without the lid on.
- Whisk in the pectin until well combined and continue to cook the mixture, stirring relentlessly, until it starts boiling.
- Boil for a minute and skim off any froth which accumulates on the surface.
- Pour it into sterilized glass jars, leaving an inch empty on top and seal them.
- Leave in the fridge to store for as long as 5 weeks.

Candied yams

Serves: 4

Ingredients:

- 2 large sweet potatoes, peeled and halved lengthwise
- 1 cup orange juice
- 1 tsp orange zest, grated
- ½ cup brown sugar
- 2 tbsp. butter
- Salt to taste

Method:

- Place the sweet potatoes into the pressure cooker and empty the cup of orange juice over them.
- Sprinkle the seasonings over it, followed by orange zest and brown sugar.
- Add a dollop of butter over the sweet potatoes and lock the cooker.

- Set timer for 7 minutes.
- Let the pressure drop speedily with the help of quick release method and open the lid.
- Strain out the sweet potatoes and place them on serving plates.
- Boil the cooking liquid further, uncovered until it thickens and spoon it over the potatoes.
- Serve as a delicious and fun side dish.

12430634R00126

Made in the USA
San Bernardino, CA
21 June 2014